The Human Self
and the
Life and Death Struggle

The Human Self
and the
Life and Death Struggle

WITHDRAWN

Piotr Hoffman

*A University of Florida/University
of South Florida Book
University Presses of Florida
Gainesville/Tampa*

University Presses of Florida is the central agency for scholarly pub-
lishing of the State of Florida's university system. Its offices are lo-
cated at 15 NW 15th Street, Gainesville, FL 32603. Works published
by University Presses of Florida are evaluated and selected for publication by a faculty editorial committee of any one of Florida's nine
public universities: Florida A&M University (Tallahassee), Florida
Atlantic University (Boca Raton), Florida International University
(Miami), Florida State University (Tallahassee), University of Central Florida (Orlando), University of Florida (Gainesville), University
of North Florida (Jacksonville), University of South Florida (Tampa),
University of West Florida (Pensacola).

Library of Congress Cataloging in Publication Data

Hoffman, Piotr.
  The human self and the life and death struggle.

  "A University of Florida/University of South Florida book."
  Bibliography: p.
  Includes index.
  1. Self (Philosophy)   2. Death.   I. Title.
BD450.H615   1984   126   83–16705
ISBN 0–8130–0778–X (alk. paper)

Printed in the U.S.A. on acid-free paper

Contents

Abbreviations

WORKS frequently cited in the text and notes have been abbreviated. Full bibliographic information is available in the reference list, which follows the notes at the end of the book.

Enc. III   G. W. F. Hegel, *Hegel's Philosophy of Mind, Part Three of the Encyclopedia of the Philosophical Sciences.*

SL   G. W. F. Hegel, *Hegel's Science of Logic.*

PhM   G. W. F. Hegel, *The Phenomenology of Mind.*

BT   M. Heidegger, *Being and Time.*

BN   J.-P. Sartre, *Being and Nothingness.*

CPR   I. Kant, *Critique of Pure Reason.*

Preface

IT IS often argued that our notion of an independent reality can emerge only when our drives, impulses, and desires encounter an obstacle. Such encounter alone, it is said, can give the subject the sense of the distinction between things as they are and things as they appear to him. In effect, when my desires are blocked by an obstacle, I come to realize that things as I wished them to be are quite different from what they are in fact, and I thus rise to the view of reality as something unaffected by my own peculiar biases and interests.

In the first chapter of this study, I advance the view that the "obstacle" here at issue—the obstacle capable of effectively blocking my pursuits and thus imposing upon me a sense of a truly independent world—can only be encountered in another man. Furthermore, I go on to argue that in order to emerge as such an obstacle, the other must be seen as an adversary (actual or at least potential) in a life and death struggle. I then try to show, in

chapters 2 and 3, how the idea of the life and death struggle can illuminate an entire cluster of issues tied up with
our notion of an independent world. In this context, I attempt to develop an account of the objectivity and freedom of the self.

The connection between the life and death struggle
and the emergence of our notion of an independent reality has been seen clearly by Thomas Hobbes, although his approach, even when supplemented with Leo
Strauss's brilliant reconstruction,[1] remains sketchy and
fragmentary. It is only with Hegel that we witness a systematic attempt to derive the notion of reality from the
life and death struggle of selves.

In chapter 5, I consider Hegel's theory in detail. In
Hegel, the life and death struggle is essentially a "battle
for ideas": the combatants engage in it in order to test a
conception each of them has of himself and of his adversary; they set out to demonstrate that they are free and
independent self-consciousnesses by risking their lives in
a battle. I argue that Hegel's idealistic account of the life
and death struggle is both impossible and unnecessary.
In order to ascend to the grasp of an independent reality,
the combatants cannot and need not be viewed as engaged in a struggle to test their self-conception. Quite
the contrary, they can and must be viewed as aiming at
the gratification of all their natural drives and impulses.
I thus take the step from idealism to naturalism, and
both the step itself and the reasons for taking it are in
conformity with a more general criticism of idealism,
which I have tried to work out in my recent book *The
Anatomy of Idealism.*[2]

But there is an important part of Hegel's overall ar-

gument in *The Phenomenology of Mind* which I think
is correct and which gains a particular relevance when
applied to the issue of the life and death struggle. I am
referring here to Hegel's famous conception of "recollection" (*Erinnerung*), a conception that allows us to understand why it is that human individuals need not go
through the process of actual struggle in order to rise to
the view of a truly independent world. The life and death
struggle is but a stage in the emergence of our form of
life. Because we are still conditioned and shaped by that
part of our heritage—internalized in the "recollection"
we have of it—we can grasp the notion of independent
reality without actually participating in the life and
death struggle.

Chapter 4 deals with two philosophers, Heidegger
and Sartre, whose positions, even though less important
to this study than the views of Hegel, are still relevant to
it. In chapter 4, I shall be arguing that Heidegger's theory of human "being toward death" is unable to account
for the very phenomena Heidegger sets out to account
for, and I shall argue that this failure must be seen as a
result of Heidegger's implicit separation of human sense
of death from the experience of human struggle. Sartre,
in my view, commits the opposite mistake: while he has a
clear conception of the struggle of selves, he fails to construe it as the life and death struggle. Consequently, he
too is unable to account for the phenomena it was his
stated goal to account for: he cannot explain how the
other can emerge as the limit of my freedom. Thus, with
the aid of some independent arguments and criticisms, I
shall be trying to reinforce in chapter 4 my earlier thesis
that the life and death struggle is at the root of man's

sense of both his death and his limitation by other men—
and hence also of his sense of an independent reality.

This book bears the stamp of long discussions with Hu-
bert L. Dreyfus, my friend and former colleague at the
University of California, Berkeley, Philosophy Depart-
ment. Without Bert's penetrating and challenging criticisms I would not have achieved whatever clarity I have
managed to find in presenting the ideas argued for in this
study. There are other debts to be acknowledged. A con-
versation with Charles Taylor helped me to clarify an important aspect of my position. Andrzej Rapaczynski's
comments induced me to make several changes in the
manuscript. Finally, Paul D. Eisenberg, who was the
reader for the University Presses of Florida, sent me an
impressive list of errata meant to correct the language of
the first draft.

Chapter 1

Struggle and Objectivity

As man finally prepares to assume his dominion over the earth, his power relationship with other men remains unchanged. For what happens when I confront a human adversary? Whatever I can use against him, he can use against me. This is not merely a factual but indeed a conceptual truth. Since my adversary—the other—is another me, his powers and abilities (his brain and his muscle, his skill and his insight) are a duplication of my own, and the same goes for the weapons each of us can throw into the battle. The sword that I raise against him, the rifle that I aim at him, the missile that I launch are matched by his sword, his rifle, and his missile. Can I still secure my victory by relying upon the sheer strength of my will? Can I hope that the other will fail to go to the brink due to fear or failure of nerve? Possibly. But then again, I should not forget for a moment that my adversary is another me. Whatever I am capable of, he is capable of too. Instead of submitting in fear, he may very well

1

choose to confront me, thereby proving that his will to
fight is not weaker than mine.

What we are witnessing here is a play of similarity
and difference, continuity and discretion. My adversary
is a genuine "other"; he is not me, he is distinct from me.
This is why he can always emerge as being in my way; he
can be an obstacle, a roadblock for me. However, unlike
a wild animal or a brute force of nature, he is an obstacle
of a very peculiar sort. His generic identity, his similarity with me make his distinctness an insurmountable
one. Since the other is another me—my mirror copy, my
alter ego—there is nothing that I can use against him
that he cannot also use against me. Everything that I
can marshall for my struggle with him, he can marshall
for his struggle with me. Thus, when I rise to confront
him, all my powers and abilities appear vulnerable; I can
never count on them with a total confidence, for their
strength can always be matched and checked by the
powers and abilities of the other. The threat from the
other is a radical one in that it can never be neutralized
and put to rest by any available and possible means at
my disposal as long as my adversary remains a member
of my own species, as long as he is generically identical
with me.

This is why the essence of the human conflict is special. It differs clearly and conceptually, not just factually,
from man's relation to organic and inorganic nature. Although nature too has tested and continues to test the
powers of man, still it makes perfect sense to talk about
progress in the human domination of nature as man's
mastery of the natural environment has now become a
fact of life. There is and there can be no such "progress"
in one's capacity to dominate a human adversary. As

Hobbes put it, "From . . . equality of ability, ariseth equality of hope."[1] To be sure, this famous passage of *Leviathan* focuses upon human adversaries' equality of hope—not of hopelessness. But it is simply the other side of the coin. If my abilities and hopes are only equal to those of the other, then it would be entirely hopeless for me to aim at bringing him under my power and control. So, according to Hobbes, the only rational choice open to me is to aim not at victory over the other but at the suspension of warfare through the "articles of peace."

Let us draw some general conclusion from these remarks. (Instead of speculating about the other's intentions and motivations and thus assuming some particular cause of human conflict, we shall focus strictly upon the other's capabilities.) Let us take a human agent—any human agent—as he pursues his goals through certain strategies, relying upon the powers at his disposal. Suppose I am this agent and the other emerges in my way. He is between me and my goals; I must remove him in order to fulfill them. What happens then?

We now have the elements needed to answer this question. Since there is nothing that can work for certain against a human adversary, I experience separation from everything I pursue. A drought that destroys my crop or a bankruptcy of the company in which I hold stocks spells the ruin of one of my strategies but does not mean an irrevocable end to my pursuits. I can still make a comeback by investing with a different company, or by opening a small business of my own, or by winning big at a casino. Moreover, even if all the strategies within my range do collapse, I can always change my goals: if I cannot be a millionaire, I can always become a dropout and hit the roads of California. However, no such escape route is possible when the other is in my way. No matter what goal I choose, he can always prevent me from realizing it; and no matter what strategy I choose to achieve my goal, he will always be in a position to block that strategy. Since his powers are equal to mine, I can count on nothing to give me a guaranteed advantage over him.

The collapse of my strategies and goals due to the emergence of an unbending human adversary signifies the collapse of my determinate, personal self and the emergence of an "objective" I. For if the other is in my way, if all of my pursuits are blocked and the realization of all of my goals is suspended in the air, my entire personal life begins to appear to be put under a gigantic question mark, which cannot be erased by any means or powers at my disposal. The first step toward self-objectification has been taken as I am suddenly forced to realize that the self I identified with may be about to collapse under the blows of the other. Here is the real root of an attitude that transforms the personal self into an object among other objects displayed under the gaze of an objective and impartial ego. Thus (we shall return to this subject later on) the objective attitude is not an outgrowth of the self's autonomous powers: it is forced upon it by the radical threat of the other. This does not mean that the withdrawal from the personal self toward the objective attitude must always be triggered by an encounter with a human enemy. Our point implies only that the capacity to adopt the objective attitude could not have emerged without the realization of a threat from a human adversary. Only such a threat can impose upon me a view of reality in which my personal self does not define me anymore since I am forced to envision its collapse and hence to establish my distinctness from it.

In order to fulfill this function of separating me from my goals and purposes, from my entire personal life, the other's power must have one quality that we have not yet mentioned. The other must emerge as a threat to all of my purposes and hence also to my purpose of staying alive. In other words, his threat must appear to be a mortal threat, for if it did not, I could still quietly and naïvely identify with at least one goal I have: surviving. Even if I were forced to abandon all the other goals I pursue, I would still have a sense of feeling myself at one with my life and with that which nourishes it: the bread that I eat, the water that I drink, and the air that I breathe. This would still remain one route open to me.

But the other is a mortal threat to me. This proposition is not posited hypothetically in order to fill the gap in the argument. His appearance in my life spells my death, for he is my alter ego, he is myself-outside-me. My life is exposed and vulnerable for the simple reason that against myself—even if appearing outside me—I have no weapons and powers to rely upon. With a gun, I can repel an attack of a grizzly bear; with a bulldozer, I can dam a creek flooding my farm. But the other aims at me what I aim at him. My faculties are strained to the breaking point, but so too are his, and they are not inferior to mine. Neither can such inferiority be found in the weapons he turns against me, for they are also my weapons. And his will and determination can be read in the steely eye that confronts me. There is nothing that can guarantee my life, and the possibility of annihilation becomes real to me.

Under the other's radical and total threat, the notion of objectivity begins to take shape. The death that the other imposes upon me spells the end of all my strategies and pursuits. Of course, I can approach my death through various strategies (courage, resignation, despair), but these strategies are merely different ways in which I approach the ultimate end of all my strategies. Against my wishes and desires, especially the desire to persist in being, the inexorable weight of reality begins to assert itself. My thinking is no longer merely wishful.

But, one could object, there is an inconsistency here. We have been insisting all along that it is the other who puts an end to my strategies; we are now saying that this power is to be attributed to my death. Now, even if it were granted that the other could not signify such an ultimate end of all my strategies and goals without representing a mortal threat to me, it would still not follow that the sense of my death could not have reached me without the other—through the permanent possibility of disease, accident, or simply old age.

The answer to this objection hinges upon our differences with Heidegger, and it will be worked out in detail later on in our systematic discussion of Heidegger's view of human "being toward death." But in order to put to rest the objection we have just formulated, we shall provisionally state our position on the issue. First of all— and here we are in complete agreement with Heidegger— it is not the case that the sense of one's own mortality here at issue (the sense of death as one's ultimate end) could ever be derived from the observation of the death of others. Death for us, as for Heidegger, means an a priori conception of oneself as mortal and finite, as running always toward the possibility of not having any possibilities. The sense of oneself as mortal is built into the overall structure of human subjectivity, instead of being formed through empirical observation of what goes on in the world, with its hospitals, morgues, and cemeteries. But—and this is where we shall disagree with Heidegger—that inner sense of the subject's own mortality and vulnerability is inseparable from his constant sense of being already exposed to the danger of an attack by the other. As we just said, this sense of exposure is not a result of an empirical generalization either. I know beforehand what it means to be exposed to the powers of the other for I know him as another me. I therefore need no empirical observation and no inference by analogy to know that his threat to me is a mortal one. Thus death is encountered inside me, but it is encountered there only because of my sense of exposure to the power of the other. In order to develop such an inner understanding of my death I must have a sense of having a *limit*, and I can only find such a limit in a *power* that limits me; in a power, that is, which I am (or may be) at the mercy of. The other is such a power.

Let us return to the notion of objective reality. In revealing himself as my ultimate end (as the end of all my strategies, goals, and desires), the other gives me the sense of objective reality. The collapse of all the aspirations and strivings of my personal self is due to an immovable object, an obstacle. This obstacle, the other, is what establishes the difference between the enchanted realm of my personal self and the hard reality that stands in my way. As long as there is something—anything—that I can count on in my struggle with this or that obstacle, I have not yet experienced the full weight of an independent world; I am still leading a semisolipsistic life in which my surroundings are malleable to my will and my desires. The other changes all that. It is he who limits me and who breaks down my initial solipsism. Nothing else could actually *do* it: not nature, which I can master or hope to master, not gods that I can defy, not some "ego-ideal" or some "higher self" (as if I couldn't always cast it aside), not the social pressures and imperatives that I am certainly free to repudiate if I only wish to do so. The other, the I-myself-outside-me, is the only obstacle in my way that can *force* me to break down the attachment to my wishes and desires. With his sword, he draws the line for me and tells me: so far and no farther. The realm of objective experience has emerged.

When we talk about objective experience or even simply "experience" *tout court*, meaning by it a fully developed mental life of an adult, we normally imply that part of what is involved in a subject's ability to have such an experience is his capacity to discriminate between his own perceptions of something and the something that is so perceived, between things as they (correctly or not) *appear* to him and things as they *are*. We can now begin to see how this difference between my view of things and things as they are or might be independently of me is introduced in the subject's mental life through an encounter with the other's radical and insurmountable threat. In experiencing the blockage of all of my wishes and desires, in seeing the collapse of the world as I represented it to myself, I realize that my representations run against the wall of something radically distinct from them. I thus posit the realm of my representations at one end of the cognitive act and the objective reality at the other end.

This objectifying role of the other's total threat to me can be made more vivid by looking at one particular way of formulating the notion of objectivity, and that is the way first explored by Kant in his *Refutation of Idealism*. The approach can be summarized as follows. In order to gain the notion of objective reality, the subject must come to view his own self as a particular item within the world. Only when I have a sense that my mental life does not encompass everything that I encounter in my career as a perceiver and an agent, only when my own self is recognized by me as being simply one piece of the furniture of the world, do I rise to the thought of objective reality. Now in order to see myself as such a particular, limited entity, distinct from other such entities, I must come to see it as being set in space, for, as Kant put it, "in order that certain sensations be referred to something outside me (that is, to something in another region of space from that in which I find myself) . . . the representation of space must be presupposed" (*CPR*, A23, B38). And thus my self, with all its mental states and experiences, becomes a particular item in the world only when I succeed in conceiving it as a spatial and hence as an embodied self. (This view need not imply some version of the mind-body identity theory. What it does imply is merely that the ascription of mental predicates—of expressions referring to thoughts, feelings, recollections, anticipations, and so on—to an entity S requires that S be construed as a bearer of physical qualities as well.) I am now in a position to identify myself as moving along a specific spatial route that is different from the routes of all other objects and that thereby allows me to draw sharp boundary lines between what belongs to the realm of my own mental experience and what goes on outside it. The self's representations are not in danger of being confused with what is given *in* them, for my pres-

ent conceptual framework allows me to distinguish between the entire landscape of the world on the one hand
and what this world looks like from a series of positions
that my self occupies as it moves along its spatial trajectory within the world. At each stage of that trajectory
the world does appear different to the self, but these
changing faces of the world are simply so many different
views of one and the same independent environment
viewed from different positions. More than that. Since I
can easily imagine how this particular percipient and
agent that I am could have taken an altogether different
route in the same spatial environment, I come to realize
that the latter would remain the same even though my
entire trajectory—and hence also all my perceptions—
would have been totally different. This experiment in
imagination serves to sharpen the line drawn between
my own perceptions and the objective world.

But how precisely do I form such a view of my embodied self, a view which allows me to survey the map of
the world and to consider my own self as a dot moving
along one of the many trajectories (actual or possible)
marked on the map? To answer this question we must
first recall what we said earlier about the emergence of
the objective, impartial attitude. It is the other who severs the link that I entertain with my personal self, and
nothing is changed if we now add that this self is an embodied self and not simply a system of purely mental appetitions and representations. In other words, in order
to objectify my body—in order to consider it as simply
one particular item in the world of objects—I must have
a sense of a mortal threat from the other. In effect, when
confronted with such a radical and total threat, I am
forced to watch my body—and hence my embodied self—

becoming exposed to the possibility of destruction in a world that would not be destroyed with it, in a world, that is, that lies beyond the limits of my body. The conception of my body's distinctness from the world with its entire furniture is imposed upon me by a power—the other's power—that does not allow me to cling to the illusion that my body is safe. Power there must be, for the emergence of the objective attitude is dependent upon the presence of an immovable obstacle to all my strivings, efforts, and desires. Only if I confront this kind of power do I realize that there is nothing I can do to prevent my body from emerging as a limited, particular entity, a realization that leads at once to the view of objective reality as something that lies beyond the limits of my psychophysical self.

We must now respond to an important objection that some contemporary philosophers would be almost certain to raise immediately against our position. Many contemporary thinkers pride themselves on having overcome and dissolved conceptual difficulties of traditional "contemplative" philosophy by establishing the priority of man's *practical* attitude toward the world. Objectivity, it is argued, has nothing to do with the uninterrupted existence of some merely "material objects" or "things-with-properties" displayed to the gaze of an uninvolved observer. An entity is objective to the extent to which it performs in a steady and reliable way a definite function in the environment of an active human subject. Language too picks out entities not according to their physical qualities and relations but according to the use they have for the speaker: the use of the thing determines the word we will attach to it. Objectivity and linguistic reference are thus secured by the thing's practical significance to man, by its reliability as a link in a world illuminated and organized by human purposes. For example, I may not be looking at my axe now, but I do have a sense of its sitting "there," in the corner of my room, where it belongs; I take it for granted that I can always get up from my chair, pick up the axe, and chop more wood to sustain the fire slowly dying in my fireplace. No matter what happens to my present perceptions—they may or may not represent the axe, they may or may not be uninterrupted representations of it—the axe endures as the instrument of a practical task assigned to it in the light of my purposes and goals. It is only when I repress (voluntarily or not) that involved attitude, only when I step back, as it were, and begin simply to stare at things that the danger of a relapse into the private world of my representations becomes real. When, instead of using things as implements (and thus taking for granted that things are not simply bundles of my own representations) I begin to stare at them, they become slowly reduced to the status of mental contents—images of qualities, shapes, sizes as they display themselves on the screen of my consciousness.

The objection we hinted at a moment ago can now be fully formulated. It is not true, a contemporary philosopher could argue against us, that the notion of objectivity emerges only after the collapse of the subject's identification with his purposes and strategies. Quite the contrary! Since the only hope of saving the conception of objective reality is to appeal to our sense of a practical environment, which we depend upon to carry out our purposes, so then also a human subject must be conceived as firmly identified with his purposes and as ac-

tively engaged in pursuing them. Were the subject to
lack this sort of identification with his practical goals, he
would adopt a disinterested attitude toward his environment. Things would then become immediately stripped
of their practical assignments, and this amounts to saying that they would cease to play the role of the furniture
of the objective world.

There is, however, a suppressed premise here. And
the question we must now ask is quite simple. How does
a practical thing (a tool, an implement, a piece of equipment) acquire its status of objectivity? If a thing's function is assigned to it by the goals which *I* pursue, then
not much has been achieved: the significance of this axe
as I use it to chop wood for my fireplace is to serve as
means of my satisfaction. To say, now, that we ought not
to consider an isolated piece of equipment (which, one
will quickly consent, can be employed for the agent's private goals) but the entire practical world, will not advance the cause either. Suppose we were willing to grant
that the objectivity of a thing is secured not in isolation
but through that thing's connection with the whole environment: to reduce the axe to the status of an item of
my private world would imply a similar reduction of the
fire burning in the fireplace, of the wood piled up in front
of my house, of the truck that was used to bring the
wood from the forest, of the forest itself, and so on. And
such reduction could not be performed by an interested
and involved agent. But the initial difficulty is only pushed
one step farther instead of being met. For it is now the
entire practical world which may be seen as serving
merely my own purposes and goals. The organization
and the structure of that world will now reflect my aims;

wherever I go, whatever I do, I encounter only myself, since the meanings and the functions of things depend solely upon the goals I will have chosen to pursue.

It will be replied at once that both the world and its elements are public since my relation to them is shaped by rules and practices that are not of my own making and that I have incorporated simply by growing up in my culture. However, these notions will not help us here. The meaning of the negation in the phrase just used, "rules and practices that are *not* of my own making," is too weak, we contend, to account for our sense of objective reality. Obviously it is true that I do not make rules for using axes; even less do I make rules for using planes or ships or for speaking a language. But if I follow all the practices and observe all the rules simply to reach *my* aims and to enforce *my* strategies, I have not yet discovered and confronted objective reality. I am still "playing a game," for what I am doing is not essentially different from the doings of a spoiled child who conforms to all the rules of a tantrum-throwing ritual in order to bend his mother's behavior to his own aims. In this way I am still pursuing the path—for I can do it as long as that path has not been closed to me by a roadblock which I cannot remove—of cultivating my own little world. Rules and practices (including the linguistic ones insofar as my speech has not yet risen above the level of manipulation) are all absorbed into that enchanted realm of mine as so many different ways and means of achieving my own ends.

The objectivity of a practical thing will emerge once I acquire the sense of that thing's being (radically and irrevocably) not under my control. To grasp an implement's distinctness from my own purposes and desires, I must realize that no matter what I try to do, the implement may persist as an obstacle in my way instead of falling submissively into a slot I have assigned to it in my plans and strategies. But to emerge thus as "standing in my way" the practical thing must be viewed as being within the reach of a power (actual or potential) of the other. Left alone—face to face as it were—with the implement, I could always hope to fix it, to repair it, to replace it; briefly, I could always hope that the drive blocked by the implement's failure to perform could still be realized. But I can entertain no such hope when the implement's resistance to my goals is due to the power of the other. To remove that resistance, I would have to attack it at its source; but to mount such an attack would imply putting myself in a position where I can count on nothing to win the battle. I can repair the leaking roof over my attic, I can protect my house from the mud slides in the spring and the fires in the summer, I can turn it into a fortress against hungry bears on the prowl, but I have nothing in my arsenal to erase my essential vulnerability to a human attack. And it is precisely the possibility of such an attack that makes me realize that my house is truly distinct from me, that it is not "there" simply to meet my goals and purposes. Briefly, practical things *are* separable from me, for they *can* be so separated by the unmanageable power of the other.

Let us grasp the full implications of that point. To be objective, a practical thing must be able to stand in the way of all of my pursuits—including even the goal of staying alive. But such conception of a practical thing can emerge only if I begin to view the other as partner in a life and death struggle. An implement's objectivity is thus realized only when I grasp it as a *deadly weapon* in the hands of the other. The dirt road that I normally take while walking to the river will appear as truly independent from me when I begin to perceive it as a path taken by a possible human aggressor; an aggressor, that is, against whom I can build no defenses. It is then—and then only—that the road appears in its full, cold, and merciless indifference to all of my pursuits: it spells the end of me, and hence it determines me as a limited self, sharply separated from what lies beyond its boundaries.

Chapter 2

The Other and Representation

Iꜰ ᴛʜᴇ other's power is what imposes limits upon me, then the other himself cannot be reduced to a representation (or a system of representations) of mine. This does not mean that I cannot represent him or form a conception of him. The other is not an ineffable and otherworldly being; he is fully accessible to my conceptual scheme and my vocabulary. But I have a way of encountering him that is not to be understood as my forming certain representations of him. The content of this statement boils down to two points: the other is distinct from each and every representation of mine including my representation of him; and the way in which I represent him corresponds to the way he really is. Let me explain what I mean. Whatever may be the general status of all conceptions and representations that I form, the representation of the other as a deadly threat to me cannot be of my own making; it is not a product of my own cognitive strategies and choices. An existent that enforces limits

17

upon my cognition, my will, and my desire is the only existent that I am forced to represent as limiting me. But to represent the other as limiting me is to represent him precisely as what he (my alter ego) already is: a potential threat of my annihilation. I cannot claim that the other is like a good uncle who is going to fit nicely into my scheme of things; at the very best, I can pretend that he fills such a slot, a pretension from which I will be disabused as soon as he chooses to engage me in a life and death struggle. Here, then, how I *represent* an existent and how that existent *is* are in agreement. Someone could be tempted to reply that I am also compelled "by the facts" to form a certain definite and nonarbitrary representation of many other things (of rocks, trees, chairs, etc.); and, to that extent, such objective "facts" or "data" would contribute to imposing many additional and equally strong constraints upon my conceptual frameworks and representations. But even if this were true—which probably it is not—we should not forget for a moment that it is the other who imposed upon me the discipline of envisioning such objective facts and data. That capacity of the other to discipline me to reality didn't stem from any cognitive or moral claims he might have had upon me but rather from the sheer power with which he brought me to the brink of my annihilation. Thus, the other's ability to impose himself as distinct and independent from all my representations made me realize the difference between myself and something independent of me. Once I gain the sense of my representations' being limited by something outside them, I am in a position to apply that distinction beyond the special area of my relations with others: I can talk (or hope to talk) about rocks, trees, and chairs as being equally independent from my ways of representing and conceiving them.

It is essential to understand that the sense of the reality of the other—of his not being like the good uncle we have just mentioned—is conveyed to me only through the life and death struggle. As long as such a struggle does not erupt, as long as it is postponed, suspended, or diluted, the other I encounter will not break through the shell of my own representations. His distinctness from them will become toned down, perhaps even to the point of being extinguished altogether. For example, in an environment governed by the rules of bargaining, the distinctness of my adversary evaporates: if I have an adequate grasp of his needs and wants and if I can come up with the means to fill them, I can manipulate him at my will. Since he is now defined by the needs and the wants to which I hold the key, he will bend to my aims. His independence and distinctness from me collapse. As of now, he *is* the image that I have of him, and he will continue to "live up" to that image, since I have the means to keep him that way—to get him fired or financially ruined or else to give him the promotion he wants or the pay raise he needs to support his family, and so on. Conversely, even if he beats me at the bargaining game, he is still not my limit, for I can simply write off the loss and begin to "play a different game" (since I am financially ruined and thus cannot lead the life of a well-to-do citizen, I may do some readjusting and decide to become a bum or a dropout). As long as the game I play with the other is not a deadly one, the door is always open for me to pursue my strategies and goals.

On the other hand, in a life and death confrontation,

the distinctness of the other stands out. It becomes absolute, for I cannot get a grip—any grip—upon him. In this sense, the other is not only absolutely distinct from me; he is the only Absolute I can encounter. Let us recall Plato's profound point in the *Parmenides*: the absolute that I encounter (enter a relation with) becomes thereby relativized and relative to me.[1] But this paradox, with which Western metaphysics hasn't ceased to wrestle, does not apply to my relationship with a human adversary whom I face in a life and death struggle. The conception that I form of him in this situation is not relative to my self; the other enforces his distinctness from me in his capacity of a power threatening to annihilate me. It is not "up to me" to present him as such a total threat; quite the contrary, his forced emergence as totally distinct from all my representations (including my representation of him as a total threat) is the very light that illumines the difference between things as they are and things as they are relative to me.

But if the other—the absolute—is thus irreducible to my representations and conceptions, he does not thereby become something mystical and ineffable. Or, to put it still differently, from the fact that the other-absolute is distinct from my conceptions and cannot be relativized to them, it does not follow, as mystical tradition thought it did, that I can form no adequate conception of him. The other is simply another man. There is nothing ineffable about him. I can describe him quite well by picking out all of his relevant natural, social, and personal qualities. It is those very qualities, not some secret power behind them, that convey to me the sense of reality as they become mobilized against me in a life and death struggle.

But—to test a possible objection—wouldn't the sheer unpredictability of a human adversary's actions be sufficient to establish him as distinct from me? Couldn't he emerge as being beyond my grip simply on account of my inability to foresee his reactions during the struggle? I submit that the answer is no. For what, exactly, is the expression "unpredictable" supposed to mean in this context? If one intends to say that at every moment the other may change his tactics, or even his main goals and strategies, then the objection is no objection at all. For there is simply something else that "makes him tick" now, and in order to adapt my response to that new challenge I must simply find out just what it is that he is after. I may conclude, of course, that as of now, i.e., with the means and strategies presently at my disposal, I cannot yet gain control over the other. But this failure does not imply that he is uncontrollable; in fact, at the very moment that I realize the inadequacy of my means, I already gain a sense of what would be needed to match his new strategies and goals. If, on the other hand, one would like to suggest that the unpredictability of the other's conduct puts him in principle beyond my reach, then the unpredictability in question can only characterize one special decision he is capable of making: his decision to detach himself from all goals and strategies dear to him and to engage me in the head-on clash of a life and death struggle. It is in that moment alone that he escapes me, since he is willing to forgo his attachment to everything that I could possibly use to control him or to foil his own attempts to control me.

To the other's distinctness from me, we must add one more quality which can emerge only during the life and death struggle: his wholeness. As long as he does not engage me in that deadly game, my relationship with him involves only a part of his being and is therefore a partial relationship. For example, suppose I own a small business, and I hire a new employee. I cannot avoid being interested in those aspects of his situation which pertain directly to his future performance on the job: I must check his past employment record, his references; I may want to know something about his family life, and so on. Normally, I need not go any further. Even when I start having conflicts and disputes with him, our relationship is still only partial. I am now interested in the kind of means he can marshall for a legal battle with me (does he have enough money to hire a good lawyer? is the union behind him?), but I remain indifferent to everything that will not affect the outcome of the lawsuit. In contrast, a man who engages me in a life and death struggle makes me concerned about his entire being. As I perceive how he is about to mobilize against me everything he's got, all of his habits and dispositions, all the aspects of his situation become relevant to me. I must consider them all, for only by mobilizing all of them does he stand a chance against a human adversary—against his very alter ego that I am. All of a sudden, then, the slightest detail of his biography becomes of tremendous relevance to me; I must "know my enemy" in order to confront and to check his power as it aims at my destruction.

In chapter 1 we considered and rejected the suggestion that a shift away from the contemplative "representation" toward the practical "understanding" (of pieces of equipment, implements, tools, etc.) would be sufficient to account for the objectivity and distinctness of the world. We have seen that the practical environment does not become distinct from me unless I begin to view it as falling under the sway of the other's uncontrollable power and hence as made up of potential weapons of my destruction. But perhaps this shift from the contemplative to the practical attitude could prove more fruitful in accounting for the distinctness of the other.

To make this suggestion is to abandon the realm of cognitive representations and to opt instead for the "understanding of the meaning of Being" embedded in our social practices. Applied to the problem of the other, this option boils down to the claim that an active, involved human agent must always interpret himself as a social being. This is the core of Heidegger's idea of *Mitsein* (Being-with). An individual's self-interpretation always involves a conception of a role played by him; and since such a role cannot be realized (or even defined) outside of a complex network of other such roles, the individual always considers himself as standing in relation to other individuals. A shoemaker's role, for example, is defined by his relations to his suppliers, his customers, etc.; he cannot "suspend his belief" in their reality without ceasing to interpret himself as a shoemaker.

It must be emphasized that such networks of social roles are themselves established and sustained by human interpretations. In Heidegger's view *Mitsein* is an "existentiale," not a "category"; in other words, it is not a ready-made attribute, and it cannot be considered independently of how it is being shaped and defined by human agents as they participate in a determinate form of life. Just as there is no "time" and no "space" in general—there are only human ways of interpreting and living space and time—so, too, *Mitsein* is articulated by living human beings. If, then, we want to talk about the network of social roles into which a human subject is always inserted, we should keep in mind that what counts as such a network is itself determined by human interpretations. Am I going to define this network in such a way as to include in it slaves and barbarians? Or madmen? Or chimpanzees? There are no epistemic or ontological standards against which we could decide these questions once and for all. The answers will depend solely upon differing ways of interpreting our Being-with.

Now, these ways of interpreting the meaning of Being-with are not at the whim of an individual, monadic self. It is not up to me to exclude madness from civilization; it is up to that particular civilization that has made me what I am. Thus in interpreting what counts as a social network I am implicitly conforming to public practices and conventions.

But do I therefore encounter the other? It is true that as a shoemaker, I find myself, in a way, having to relate, in conformity with public rules, to my customers, suppliers, etc. But do I grasp them as truly limiting me? Not at all! I simply go through the routine of my daily activities: working, paying my suppliers, making home deliveries to my customers, and so on. In all of this, I pursue *my* strategies and goals. At no point does the other stand out. At no point does he assert himself as my true limit. To be sure, he is not my "representation" any more. Still, he is fully identical, at least as far as I am concerned, with the social slot that he occupies and that remains part and parcel of my environment (malleable to my pursuits and goals). At no point does the reality of the other invade my world. My aims toward the other are shaped by an interpretive network, but they are still my aims and the other conforms to them. He can assert himself as truly distinct from me only if he chooses to stand in my way by engaging me in a life and death struggle. At that moment alone does he cease to occupy a slot within my world. His emergence as a total threat to me signifies the possibility of annihilation of my world and is therefore the limit of the latter.

Thus nothing is changed when we move from the network of representations to the background of (pre-cognitive) interpretations. Their self-enclosed magic circles can be broken through only if the other begins to pursue my annihilation. What he then means to me—or what he "represents"—is not bestowed upon him by an interpretive network. As the irrevocable and insurmountable end of an interpretive being's strategies and pursuits, the other is not absorbed into them. Here and here only this interpretive being that I am can experience the full weight of reality. The other imposes himself upon me in that sheer innocence of an undisguised force that Rousseau and Nietzsche, each in his own way, have opposed to the masks of civilization. As a total threat to me, the other belongs to the original being. He cuts through the layer of appearance deposited by the play of interpretations and meanings. He is my death. *That* is not a mere claim he advances, or a mere role he plays.

We have been saying all along that the emergence of objective selves is due, both in the case of my self and in the case of the self of the other, to the life and death struggle between us. It is only to the extent that both of us engage in such a struggle that we are capable of rising above the level of our private individual biases and beliefs. The justification of these claims will be strengthened greatly if we can show how they could be instrumental in solving certain conceptual difficulties and puzzles generated by the traditional views of the self. Without pretending for a moment to be able to come up with a complete list of such difficulties and to offer their resolutions, I would like to focus in detail on what appears to be the major difficulty the traditional philosophizing encountered while grappling with the notion of objective self. Since the objective, impartial self must be able to step back from all the uncritical beliefs, biases, and wishes of the empirical self, it was assumed that the former must be construed as a nonempirical self. However, having deprived themselves of any right to appeal to the criteria of identity normally employed to identify a self—for such criteria arise only in the context of our need to identify the mundane, empirical personality of the subject, and they therefore could have no value beyond that original area of ordinary discourse—traditional philosophers were then confronted with a persisting "elusiveness" of the nonempirical self. Since the ordinary criteria of self's identity had to be repudiated, and since no other such criteria seemed to be available, the "pure" self was forever escaping the conceptual net of the philosopher. Yet, it was felt, such a self had to be posited in order to account for the possibility of objectively valid cognitions.

Now, if we can show that our own interpretation of the self will allow us to account for its emergence as objective without leading us into the trap of the elusive "transcendental" or "pure" I, then we will have strengthened the case for our entire interpretation.

We must first show that the difficulty we have attributed to traditional philosophical views is indeed endemic to them, and to do this we shall briefly review the positions of the most important thinkers who have had to wrestle with the issue of the nonempirical I.

Descartes is undoubtedly the first philosopher whose system brings out the difficulty of dealing with the nonempirical I. After having asserted his methodical doubt and having been left only with the certainty of "I think, therefore I am," Descartes was led, by the nature of the case, to set himself the following task: "I am seeking to discover what I am, that 'I' that I know to be."[2] But his answer—"I am a mind"—does not tell me how to identify this particular mind that I am. In fact—and this is a weakness in Descartes' position with which we are all familiar by now—there seems to be no reason at all for referring mental experiences to a particular self. First of all, it is clear that in order to pick out the referent of the expression "I," I cannot rely upon any identity criteria tied to the concept of my body. For since it is possible that what I take to be my body is in fact an illusion or a hallucination of mine, while at the same time it remains certain that I who hallucinate, dream, etc., continue to exist, it is possible for me to exist without the actual existence of what I take to be my body. From this it follows—and it does so according to Descartes himself—that it is not part of my nature to have a body. Hence the identification of that elusive "I" cannot be based upon the criteria of bodily identity. (This conclusion is in itself sufficient to show that my "I" cannot be identified at all by an external observer. In effect, such an external observer could rely only upon the knowledge of my body to identify any of my mental states. But since his methodical doubt deprives him of any way of justifying his belief in the reality of my body, he cannot identify my "I" either; in fact—and for the same reason—he does not even have the right to attribute mere existence to my self.) I must therefore fall back upon some purely mental criteria in order to secure the reference of the expression "I"—expression that I continue to employ even while adopting the attitude of the skeptic. But such purely mental criteria of the self's identity do not seem to fare much better, given the fact that the methodical doubt has suspended all beliefs based on memory. I can entertain no hope of establishing that this present mental image of a mountain is my image by relying upon its connections with my mental history. Because I have no way of telling the difference between a veridical recollection and a memory illusion, I have no way of justifying any belief about my mental history; in fact, I do not even know whether I have had such a mental history at all. I may try to solve the entire difficulty by insisting that the reference of the present mental states I am having to my own "I" must be given immediately and without any criteria in each and every first-person, present-tense report that I make. (I cannot report on my feeling of an intense pain without assuming that I am having this particular pain.) But this is simply to beg the question, at least if we adopt Descartes' conception of philosophizing. For even if it were the case that grammar forces me to employ the reference to my "I" in a certain type of report (first-person, present-tense), it would not follow that I have produced a compelling reason for that practice of ordinary thought and language. The standard criticisms of the *cogito* are irrefutable here: if I accept (as Descartes wants me to) the task of critically examining the assumptions embedded in ordinary thinking and

speaking, I have not so far given any justification for attributing certain mental states to my "I." To produce
such a justification, I would first have to produce a way
of identifying the "I" itself. And this I cannot do since I
have repudiated all ordinary criteria of the self's identity. Once such repudiation is consistently carried out,
we are left only with the impersonal sets (anonymous, as
it were) of mental states and activities.

Kant is in no better position here. He too distin-
guishes between the empirical and the nonempirical self.
We have no insurmountable problems with establishing
the criteria of identity for our empirical self. After all,
such empirical self is simply one particular item in our
objective experience, and hence it can easily be identified by means of empirical rules we normally call out in
order to identify all the other items belonging to the
world of experience. But the nonempirical self—the
"pure apperception"—is not such an item. Kant repeats
tirelessly that the pure self cannot be made into an object of knowledge, and hence it follows at once that no
empirical criteria of identity can be applied to such a self.

Now if the reference of mental states to the pure self
were only, as the *Paralogisms* suggest, a grammatical
and logical necessity, then indeed Kant would have no
problem here. He would not have to worry about the
"pure self's" identity, for he would not be claiming that
this expression refers to an entity. But, the *Paralogisms*
notwithstanding, Kant cannot and does not stop at such
a strictly formal treatment of the nonempirical self. For
him, the pure self is charged with the task of accomplish-
ing the transcendental syntheses, due to which our entire objective experience, including also our experience
of the empirical selves, first arises. The pure appercep-

tion is thus "something real" (*CPR*, B419), and it is described as a "power of combination" (*CPR*, B159). But then the "I" cannot simply be a grammatical function— we must establish its reference to some "real" and "active" self, a task that implies at once our ability to identify such a self. And this does not seem to be feasible once we abandon the empirical criteria of the self's identity; in fact, we cannot even establish the numerical differences between pure selves since the category of quantity can have no valid cognitive employment beyond the area of space and time, while the pure selves can be exhibited neither in space nor in time. The only way in which the pure selves do come within our grasp is as mere participants in the universal law-giving activity of mind, as "consciousness in general," to use the expression introduced by Kant in the *Prolegomena*. But such consciousness in general is the same in all (rational) knowers, and hence we have no way of establishing those knowers' individuality. Once again, the repudiation of empirical criteria (mental, material, or both) of a self's identity leaves us with an anonymous, impersonal consciousness. Although many commentators think that this is what Kant should have said, such a view is clearly incompatible with Kant's own repeatedly stated positions.

To conclude this review and then to offer our own solution to the problem, let us state the problem once again. In constructing an account of our ability to achieve a grasp of objective reality, the traditional philosopher must refuse to identify the knower with the latter's particular, empirical self. It is clear that such a self is always in the grip of its own untested beliefs and biases, that it considers things from its own peculiar point of view, conditioned as it is by its own history and background. Since the ability to grasp objective reality requires that the knower not be confined to such peculiarities of his empirical, determinate station in life, we must conceive him as a nonempirical (a "pure," a "transcendental") self. But by thus conceiving the subject as stripped of all of his empirical qualities, we are closing the door to all attempts at identifying and individuating him. Yet, on the other hand, he must be individuated, for the hypothesis of an anonymous, impersonal mind leads us into the undesired embraces of murky, pantheistic metaphysics.

Let us now look at what happens when the other emerges as my adversary in a life-and-death struggle. As his equal, I am for him his alter ego, his own self-outside-him. I am now the power that severs his attachment to everything he holds onto: his desires, his wishes, his beliefs. Because of the total threat that I represent to him, it is now he who emerges as an objective self. By responding to my mortal threat he is no longer taking anything for granted. He is forced to consider all of his strategies, goals, and powers as vulnerable and exposed to annihilation. He thus ascends to a grasp of reality which is not determined by those powers, strategies, and goals. He has suspended—he has been forced to suspend—his naïve, uncritical reliance upon the entire content of his determinate, personal self. But—and this is the crucial step in our argument—the newly acquired objectivity of his position does not transform him into an unidentifiable and elusive self. He is still the same man that he was before I attacked him: he is identifiable by the same qualities and dispositions, by the same life history, by the same habits and preferences. Only to the ex-

tent that I challenge the man identifiable by this specific
set of qualities, dispositions, and habits, and to the extent that he takes up that challenge, is he forced to
emerge as an objective agent and knower. The change
that has occurred in him is not a change in "what" but a
change in "how." Suppose he was identifiable by the
qualities P, Q, R. Thus the man identifiable by P, Q, R
is now forced to adopt the objective attitude. But he has
not thereby become the owner of some unique and im-
penetrable "stream of consciousness" or an elusive
"pure" ego. His new attitude is still an attitude of his—it
is simply a different way of organizing P, Q, R in their
relationship to me, to him, and to the world. Similarly,
when I am forced—by his no-holds-barred response to
my challenge—to rise to the conception of objective reality, I do not therefore cease to be identifiable by my
qualities and dispositions. The latter still define me in my
own eyes and in his eyes as well; only to the extent that I
have entered the life and death struggle I too have been
forced to adopt a different attitude toward the entire
content of my personal self.

To state the argument succinctly, I place it in the
formal mode:

1. The other rises to the level of objective attitude
not when he chooses to flee from the life and death confrontation through a withdrawal from the world into
some sheltered realm of his "pure self." On the contrary,
he rises to the level of objectivity precisely to the extent
that he becomes actively involved in a life and death
struggle with me.

2. The man—*this* man—who does not flee or submit
appears in my environment; he is a determinate person,

endowed with specific qualities that I can easily pick out in order to identify him.

3. Hence, in his capacity of a knower and agent capable of rising to the level of objectivity, the other can be identified by all the wealth of his empirical qualities.

Chapter 3

Freedom and Facticity

THE MODERN idea of freedom first arose with Descartes's and Kant's discovery of human subjectivity. Until then, philosophical thought was familiar only with the problem of "free will," a problem that was in turn part of the larger problematic of contingency vs. necessity. In philosophical discussions and arguments this problematic was defined by the following dilemma: Is it the case that propositions stating the occurrence of future events are either true or false prior to the actual occurrence of those events, or is it rather the case (as it would have to be, if the notion of contingency were to make sense) that such propositions are neither true nor false until the event in question actually does or does not occur? The entire conceptual framework for thus formulating the problem of free will can be traced to Aristotle. It is by restricting the application of the principle of excluded middle that Aristotle defends, in *De Interpretatione*, the possibility of contingent events. To take his famous ex-

34

ample: It is true today that either there will be a sea
fight tomorrow or there won't be a sea fight tomorrow;
but it is not yet true that there will be a sea fight tomorrow and it is not yet true that there won't be a sea fight
tomorrow. Even Leibniz still posed the problem in those
terms. Since God knows the complete individual essence
of Adam, the truth of all propositions about Adam's future conduct is known to God beforehand; Leibniz's difficulty was then to show how Adam could still be said to
have free will. To say the least, Leibniz's answer—the
choices fixed for Adam by God "incline without neces-
sitating"—has not been very effective in putting to rest
the doubts of his critics.

What is implied by the theories of free will constructed with the aid of such a model is that the possibilities of alternative future choices are all laid out
in advance. The agent does not create his options but
rather finds them, all fixed and ready, waiting for him to
approach them at some future date. Or the possibilities
are not of the agent's own making; they are established
and sustained by the order of things.

The modern conception of human freedom is entirely different. Its main assumption is the belief in man's
ability to break with the order of things and to create a
world for himself. Freedom, here, is identical with man's
power (his "negativity" or "projection," to use contemporary philosophical terminology) to transcend in imagination the narrow boundaries of his given position in nature and society and to follow up on those new vistas by
actively transforming the conditions of his life. Hence it
cannot be stated in advance what the possibilities that
the agent will encounter in his future are; any attempt to
determine them before they are actually posited by the

agent himself is absurd since they cannot be said to "exist" until they are first projected and mapped out by him.

In order for this creative power of human "negativity" or "projection" to be set in motion, the agent must be able to set himself apart from his entire past. To be sure, this is not the sufficient condition of human freedom, but it is its necessary condition. To say that the agent's present offers him the opportunity to create a new future for himself is to imply that he is not enslaved by his past: by his character and his habits, by his dispositions and inclinations, by his social and economic background, and so on. Already Kant had seen clearly the necessity of conceiving a truly free agent, as one who is capable of breaking away from the causal chains binding him to his past.[1]

If the arguments advanced in the earlier chapters were sound, it would have to follow that the agent could never establish himself as so radically distinct from his own past—from the personal self that he was all along—without encountering the other in a life and death confrontation. And thus, it seems, the life and death struggle must be regarded as the very condition of human freedom.

The past that I must be able to break with goes into making up what the existentialist philosopher calls my "facticity." This expression, which we shall employ in our further argument, refers precisely to my self insofar as I consider it in its fixed and established qualities, i.e., in its past. Whatever it is that I may envision for the future, I cannot change the fact that I was born with such and such mental and physical qualities which I have already put to such and such uses; I cannot change the fact that I was born with certain impulses and dispositions, or that I have developed certain habits and preferences, acquired certain skills, and so on. But nothing forces me to obey my past. I can improvise and create, I am free to lay out new possibilities—and in that capacity I break away from the causality of my past self; I establish myself as nonidentical with it, as distinct from it.

However, this ability to sever the ties with myself cannot emerge, as we saw earlier, from an inner development of my own powers. If it weren't for the deadly challenge of the other, I would remain forever comfortably immersed in my past because there would be nothing capable of forcing me to break that enchanted bond or even of giving me the very conception of such a break. This conception I owe only to the other. Because of the radical and total threat from the other, I am made to emerge as nonidentical with my factical self. That factical, given self (defined as it is by my impulses, my dispositions, my habits, my preferences, etc.) is now exposed and vulnerable to the attack of the other. There is nothing in that self that could give me a foolproof protection against the other, and hence I experience the separation, the distance from everything my factical self is. I cannot simply fall back upon my impulses, my dispositions, or my habits, for I cannot depend upon them to repulse the attack of the other. This alone breaks up the naïve solidarity that I felt with my factical self. Since I can take nothing for granted in my struggle with the other, I must always be prepared to break with the established pattern of my impulses, dispositions, propensities, and habits. Whatever I am in my facticity is now left behind, like a fortress that I found myself compelled to abandon since I knew it couldn't offer me protection. I am forced to break with my past and to map out new ways of living my life because to let myself be locked within the boundaries of my factical self (to follow passively my impulses, dispositions, and habits) would be tantamount to signing my death warrant. This fixed self of mine that the other threatens with annihilation cannot be "all" I am; or rather, through the same stance that I refuse my annihilation at the hands of the other, I must establish myself as distinct from the self that the other *can* annihilate.

But this is only part of the story. Human freedom is a situated freedom, and what defines that situatedness is supplied by my factical self. I am capable of breaking with my past and of laying out and "projecting" new possibilities; but a possibility that has no bonds with my factical self is not a real possibility of mine; rather, it is a fantasy or a mere thought. Clearly, I cannot aim at winning the Olympics if I lack the necessary skills and dispositions. Thus my factical self is myself after all. Whatever I project and intend to accomplish, I must do so in terms of my own factical background. But how can we make sense of this play of identity and difference within the self? How can I both *be* and *not be* my factical self?

Let us begin to answer this question by noting the following. It is one thing to advance a philosophical claim to the effect that freedom and facticity are both essential components of human agency. It is quite another thing to explain how (and why) it is that the agent himself realizes and acts out such a view of his condition. What makes the agent come to terms with his factical self? Why does he assume and acknowledge the latter instead of living in the imaginary realm of his thoughts and fantasies? If we can find some answer to these questions we shall be in a position to solve the entire puzzle: how can I both be and not be my factical self?

We can see already that the puzzle (I am and I am not my factical self; I accept it and I refuse it; I identify myself with it and I set myself apart from it) cannot be solved without adopting some form of the "dialectics of selfhood." And since we are thus squarely committed to the view of the self as a dialectical unity of identity and difference, it seems natural and useful to begin our search for a solution by consulting the writings of the founder of modern dialectics.

Hegel has indeed confronted the entire puzzle. For him the facticity of the self, what he calls the self's "being" or "reality," provides the necessary background of freedom. In all of his analyses, Hegel emphasizes that the agent's aims and purposes (the possibilities laid out by the power of his "negativity") can be realized only within the setting of his social station, his tradition, his impulses, his habits, his dispositions, and so on. To be sure, the pure I cannot lack the capacity to break all the bonds with its factical position—pure "negativity" can thus set itself apart from "being"—but this capacity is only necessary, not the sufficient, condition of a genuinely free human conduct. The latter can take place only if the self accepts and acknowledges its factical limits. There can be no doubt that the notion of "situated freedom" is present in the rich world of Hegel's philosophical ideas.

I have argued elsewhere that Hegel's aim of reconciling the "negativity" of pure self with its "reality" (i.e., with the self's determinate, empirical content) cannot be carried out with the aid of Hegel's own idealistic (and still much too Kantian) conceptual framework.[2] Here I would like to focus, in a similar vein, upon Hegel's intention to work out a theory of situated freedom.

In an important section of his *Science of Logic*, Hegel spells out just how we ought to think about the pure self in order to see it as firmly bound up with all of its determinate, natural and social, qualities (*SL*, 775–83). His hope is to show that the formal "I think" of Kant, when properly conceived, will of itself exhibit its connection with the manifoldness of the given empirical content. It is this hope, I believe, which remains unfulfilled in spite of Hegel's efforts.

Let us summarize in a few words Hegel's own summary of Kant's position (*SL*, 776–78). According to Kant, there can be no cognitively valid ascription of any predicates to the pure "I" taken as the mere form of our representations. Since it is the very condition of all my representations, the "I" itself cannot be made into a representation and hence cannot be grasped by means of predicates applicable to representations. If I tried to form and to determine the representation of my I, it would still be my I who would be forming that representation, and thus the I representing itself would not be identical with the I represented; we could apply all kinds of predicates to the latter, but none to the former. From this, Kant draws his well-known conclusion: our conception of pure "I" must remain absolutely empty; the pure I is here only an "x," as Hegel puts it, which must be posited as the necessary form of all representations. And this is the very position that Hegel sets out to demolish in the *Science of Logic*. Far from its being the case, he suggests, that the necessary reference of the I to itself (in forming a representation of my "I" it is still *I* who am forming that representation) is a vicious circle or an "inconvenience," this self-referring quality of the ego opens up the possibility of avoiding its merely formal treatment. Hegel's argument has basically three steps. First, to say that my I is implicated in each and every one of my representations amounts to saying, in full agreement with Kant, that in all of my representations I remain identical with myself; in all of them "I am I." Second, the statement "I *am* I" includes the reference to the pure self's being, to its reality.[3] This, again, is fully supported by Kant's own doctrine: "in the consciousness of myself in mere thought I am the *being itself*" (*CPR*, B429). But third, what do we mean when we talk about the "being" of the self? We intend to signal, Hegel insists, that the self is something actual, real, that it is not just some shadowy conception. But the reality of the self can be found only in the self's natural and social setting. In order to gain its reality, the life of my I must be embodied and expressed—in my habits, in my impulses, in my speech, in my social role. In other words, to talk about the I as existing—which is exactly what we do while stating the initial principle "I *am* I"—implies a conception of it as displaying itself in the full diversity of its content. And thus starting with the pure form of "I" we discover in it the "empirically perceptible" wealth of content: "It is this relationship through which, in immediate self-consciousness, the absolute, eternal nature of self-consciousness and the Notion itself manifests itself for this reason, that self-consciousness is just the *existent* pure *Notion*, and therefore *empirically perceptible*, the absolute relation-to-self" (*SL*, 777). To this third step in Hegel's argument, as we have reconstructed it here, a Kantian would reply at once that in order to thus "empirically perceive" the spiritual life of a pure self one must be able to exhibit the latter in an intuition; but this is not possible because we have no way of exhibiting the pure self in the sensible intuition conditioning our experience. But Hegel meets this objection head-on: "If external intuition, determined in space and time, is required for objectivity, and it is this that is missing here, then it is quite clear that by objectivity is meant merely sensuous reality; and to have risen above *that* is the condition of thinking and of truth" (*SL*, 778). And, in effect, Hegel's entire philosophical effort can be seen as focused upon the task of articulating the sort of (non-sensible) "intuition" we rely upon in our study of the world of spirit.

We can now return to the question we asked at the beginning: what is it that leads the I itself to acknowledge and to assume its factical self? Hegel is acutely aware of the importance of this sort of question: in the Introduction to *The Phenomenology of Mind*, we are told in no uncertain terms that we should never be satisfied with a merely philosophical claim; we must always show how such a claim is supported by the experience of the prephilosophical, "natural" subject. How, then, do I discover my identity with my factical self?

Hegel's answer is simple. I am led to acknowledge and to assume my factical self once I come to realize the failure of the opposite strategy: the strategy of denial. When Hegel outlines his view of such a strategy of denial in the *Philosophy of Right*, he describes it as leading into the blind alley of the "fury of destruction."[4] If I attempt to act without carefully taking into account the limitations of my factical self—my biological needs, my habits, my social and economic situation, etc.—I cannot build anything; I can only destroy. This "freedom of the void" is an individual counterpart of that collective experiment in destruction that Hegel saw in a revolutionary terror aiming at the realization of some utopian ideals unconnected with the existing social practices, traditions, and institutions.[5] I must come to terms with and set myself within my factical self for the very simple reason that I must actualize my aims and conceptions, and no such actualization can be achieved by the display of that fantastic "abstract" form of freedom—as defined by its power of denial of facticity.

Thus the agent is led to acknowledge and accept his own facticity through his recognition of the failure of a strategy. The subject, that is, comes to understand that the strategy of abstract, merely negative freedom is burdened by an inner contradiction since the purpose of actualizing the self is incompatible with the refusal to acknowledge and to take up the self's facticity, its determinateness.[6]

But we must address here against Hegel an objection sustained by the same logic as the main criticism with which his system has been met in the writings of existentialist philosophers. If the acknowledgment of my facticity is due only to my recognition of the failure of a strategy (abstract freedom turns out to be a one-sided and incomplete notion), then I am free to persist indefinitely in refusing to come to terms with my factical self. Since the agent has a perfect "choice"[7] in that matter, he can always avoid the responsibility of facing up to his recognition that the strategy of abstract freedom is a failure; or, to put it another way, he can decide not to live up to his own (deeper and better) understanding of what it means to be a truly free agent. What is missing in Hegel's purely *conceptual* dialectic of the self is the notion of an *existential experience* capable of undercutting the subject's stubborn attachment to a one-sided way of interpreting and realizing his freedom.

Considered from this perspective, Kierkegaard's treatment of self represents a great progress. Furthermore, since Kierkegaard's solution to our problem provides the paradigm of all future existentialist solutions, we shall focus upon it in some detail.

In *The Sickness Unto Death*, Kierkegaard describes the human self as composed of a set of pairs of "factors": the infinite and the finite, the eternal and the temporal, the possible and the necessary. The expression "composed" may be misleading here: the factors are not to be understood as some ready-made attributes or qualities of the human self; rather they are (for that self) tasks to be coped with, problems to be solved. And thus, for example, it is impossible to state "what" man's need of the eternal "is" without taking into account how man interprets that need, how he relates it to his need of the temporal, and so on. Now, most forms of selfhood are characterized by a "disrelationship" of the factors—by the attitudes, that is, in which the assertion of one kind of need is bought at the price of repressing the opposite need. Such a "disrelated" self is described as leading the life of despair. Now, the one form of the self's disrelationship pertaining directly to our concerns is the disrelationship between Necessity and Possibility. Both belong equally to the self, and they embody the play of being and non-being, of reality and negation. "Inasmuch as [the self] is itself, it is necessary, and inasmuch as it has to become itself, it is a possibility."[8] However, in its first impulse to realize its need of possibility, the self takes a stand relegating necessity to the status of something irrelevant. The self becomes thus "an abstract possibility";[9] the subject begins to live in fantasies and mere thoughts, totally oblivious to reality. The aspect of factical self is passed over: nothing is seen as imposing limits and constraints upon the subject's aims. But then those aims become purely imaginary. Since everything is possible to me, nothing becomes truly actual: my self has become a "fantastic" self. In order to realize my aims I must concern myself with *real* possibilities, and these can only be laid out by an agent capable of assuming his factical, limited self and of relying upon the latter's powers in the pursuit of his dreams and ideals.

Were we to ask Kierkegaard what it is that would make a man recognize and assume this task of coming to terms with his factical self, his reply would not be based on a merely conceptual dialectic of selfhood. The agent gains the sense of one-sidedness and sterility of his "fantastic" self not through a grasp of some reasons but in an existential experience. This experience is despair. Despair is the mood which grips a "disrelated" self. As long as the agent's projection of possibilities will not be balanced by reconciliation with necessity, his self will be consumed by despair. And this experience "softens up," as it were, the agent's stubborn attachment to abstract possibilities; it makes him receptive to the acceptance of necessity.

Where we shall take issue with Kierkegaard's solution is where he himself would probably see its main strength. In Kierkegaard's view, despair is a "sickness," but not a sickness that "befalls" a man.[10] In a sense, despair is a self-induced sickness. Its appearance is due to the agent's own self-interpretation. Despair flows from the strategy he has chosen to cope with the human predicament. True, the choice is here not a deliberate one; quite the contrary, it determines all volitions and deliberations of the agent. In fact, the choice does not even have to be "conscious," at least not in the ordinary sense of that term. Still, the mood of despair grips an individual only because he himself commits and recommits his self to a certain way of life. In effect, the very reason that one's despair is a sickness unto *death* is to be found in despair's dependence upon that deep choice of one's entire way of life. Because we are not dealing here with deliberate volitions, the self cannot, by its own will, manipulate itself out of despair; and because we are dealing here with the self's own choice, no external change can ever free the self from the state of despair. The change— if there ever will be one—will have to come from a change in the individual's way of interpreting and living the human condition.

It is thus clear that the self may in principle persist indefinitely in its attachment to the "fantastic" life of mere possibilities and thoughts. This conclusion should not come as a surprise to us, for if the drama of existential despair is all played out on the stage of human self-interpretations, it is up to the actor to continue in his role—whatever that role might be. Since nothing *forces* him out of it—or can at least be envisioned as in principle capable of doing so—he is free to pursue that particular strategy he has devised for dealing with the human condition. And even if we were to grant Kierkegaard that the grace of God could open for me the path of reconciliation of both sets of factors (and hence "cure" my despair), it would still be up to me either to refuse or to accept that divine gift.

Nothing is changed in this picture if the Kierkegaardian despair is supplemented by guilt.[11]

How, then, do I finally acknowledge and come to terms with my factical self? Why am I not free to deny my limitations indefinitely through a strategy of opting for the life in the imaginary realm of mere possibilities? What is it that would be in principle capable of compelling me to abandon that strategy? The answer is not difficult to guess. In order to be able to continue with my strategies and goals, I cannot adopt a strategy leading to the end of all strategies and goals that I pursue. To be more specific: If the refusal of my factical self amounts to the acceptance of my annihilation at the hands of the other, I must—for I am forced to—acknowledge and come to terms with my factical self. But why would the avoidance of my factical self mean the path of annihilation for me, especially since—as pointed out earlier—it is the factical self that makes me vulnerable and hence must be left behind?

The answer is in the question. For the same reason that I cannot afford to identify myself with that factical self, I cannot afford not to identify myself with it. The threat of destruction at the hands of the other reaches me via the threat to my factical self. If this self—with all its social and natural qualities—dies, I shall die too. We argued this point at the end of chapter 2: both combatants are identifiable not by being bearers of some "pure

egos" but by their empirical, mundane qualities. To kill
the man with this particular description (the man with
such and such background, dispositions, habits, etc.) is
to kill me. In order to comprehend this I do not need any
inference. At the very moment that I recognize the vulnerability of my factical self, I recognize my vulnerability. If I continue to ignore this recognition—if I thus
continue to live as a "fantastic" self immersed in mere
possibilities—I shall be doing it at the risk of inviting my
own annihilation. I must acknowledge and take up my
factical self, for this is a matter of life and death for me.

Moreover, this acknowledgment of my factical self is
not only a liability but an asset as well. As pointed out
earlier, in my response to the other's challenge I must set
myself apart from my past and aim at the fulfillment of
new possibilities. This ability to improvise and to change
offers me a chance to escape the other's deadly embrace.
But I can hope to realize my possibilities only if they
show some connection with the powers of my factical
self: with my drives and my dispositions, with my train-
ing and my skill. Now the task of realizing my possibilities is not—not as we interpret it in the present
study—some vague urge to "actualize" the self or to escape the feelings of guilt or despair. The task—and this
is why I must respond to it—is simply to avoid my annihilation. A possibility which I do not realize is not a
weapon in the very real struggle I must wage against the
other. I must identify with my factical self because I
need all its powers in order to realize my possibilities,
and I cannot afford not to realize them—not unless I am
prepared to accept the annihilation of all my possibilities.

I cannot afford to be my (factical) self and I cannot
afford not to be it. I cannot afford to be my factical self,

for that factical self is about to be annihilated by the other; to sink into total identity with my factical self is to give up on my very *life*. The possibility of such strategy is always open to me, but it is the possibility of terminating all my strategies. Therefore, as long as I want to continue this adventure called "me" I am forced (due to the total and radical threat of the other) to break away from the causal chains binding me to my factical self; I am forced to search for new ways and new lands; I am forced to lay out and explore possibilities that would put me beyond the reach of the other's power. But such exploration is freedom. I am thus "forced to be free"—to use a famous phrase—by the deadly seriousness of the other's threat to me. By the same token and because of the same pressure, my freedom is made to set itself within my facticity. Thus I cannot afford not to be my factical self. If it weren't for the other's threat, I could remain immersed forever in my fantasies and my dreams or I could go on and on acting out some utopian ideals. But the other makes me *confront* my factical self. By refusing my destruction at his hands I must accept and acknowledge that self.

Of this conjunction of freedom and facticity no conceptual or existential dialectic of selfhood will ever be able to give an account. As long as we remain on the level of human self-interpretations, freedom does not find the weight that ties it down to facticity. A conceptual conflict or tension can continue unresolved because I can always refuse to follow up on the dialectical implications and ramifications of my thought. Similarly, I can refuse to enter the hard and tortuous path of living up to the deepest meaning that I myself (or my culture) proclaim to be the human condition. Nothing short of the life and death struggle will put an end to such strategies. For in that struggle the veil of conceptions and interpretations is pierced by the power of the other. Whatever is necessary to allow me to respond to that deadly threat cannot be denied and interpreted away.

Chapter 4

Death and Struggle: Heidegger and Sartre

W E SHALL concentrate here on Heidegger's interpretation of man's sense of death and on Sartre's phenomenology of the human conflict. There is an interesting symmetry to be noted. Heidegger considers death in
separation from struggle, while for Sartre the struggle
of selves shows no links whatever with the experience of
mortality. These are matters crucial to our argument.
Death without struggle, struggle without death; both
positions, we shall argue, are profoundly one-sided and
hence unable to account for the phenomena.

For Heidegger, the analysis of man's sense of his death
represents the crucial stage in the existential analytic of
Dasein and indeed in the fundamental ontology itself.
Heidegger's ultimate aim in *Being and Time* is not sim-

ply to describe this or that item in the structure of *Da-sein* or even to come up with a hermeneutical interpreta-tion of the totality of such items. From the beginning, Heidegger defines his purpose as much more ambitious: he intends to proceed with an inquiry (fundamental on-tology) into the meaning of being in general. He then takes two steps that give his analysis of death the para-mount importance that it enjoys in *Being and Time*. First, the inquiry into the meaning of being in general presupposes a clarification of the meaning of being of *Dasein*—of man considered in his unique status of a self-interpreting entity. This step is justified by one single ar-gument. Man, for Heidegger, is a being-in-the-world. Thus in interpreting himself—in taking a stand on what it means to be human—man *eo ipso* interprets the mean-ing of reality in general. That is, the way in which man views reality (what counts as real to him, his "world") depends upon how he views himself. Since the meaning of being in general is thus shaped and articulated by *Da-sein*, we must understand the latter in order to gain ac-cess to the former. Second—and this is the step that Heidegger takes at the beginning of division two of *Being and Time*—if the project of fundamental ontology is to be completed, we must have a way of arriving at the ultimate understanding of the meaning of being. We have already noted that being is made intelligible in the attitudes and stances of human *Dasein* as *Dasein* inter-prets the meaning of its own being. It follows that the ultimate grasp of the meaning of being in general can be achieved only if we succeed in uncovering the ultimate (the "primordial") structure of *Dasein*. As long as we are not familiar with *Dasein*'s ultimate structure, we are in darkness about what makes *Dasein* interpret itself, and hence also being in general. Now, one condition that must be met if we are to be in a position of clarifying *Dasein* in its ultimate structure is that we must be able to achieve not this or that partial view of *Dasein* but a view of it as a whole. But, the argument continues, *Dasein* becomes a whole only in its death (*BT*, 280). An individual's past and present life acquire their meaning only in the light of goals and purposes ("possibilities") that this individual aims at. Therefore, as long as the individual is alive—as long as he lays out and pursues ever new possibilities—his identity is not a "settled" matter. It is open to constant reappraisal and reinterpretation. A new selection of goals may force a radical revision of what we took to be that individual's character and identity. We may be forced to admit that he was not what he "appeared" to be because his new choice of possibilities is incompatible with the conception we had of him for a number of years. Only in death is *Dasein* finally *defined*. With death, nothing remains "unsettled" and "outstanding": the last sentence in the individual's biography has been written, and the book of his life is now displayed for final inspection. Only death can thus puncture the network of self-interpretations, for death spells the end of the self-interpretive activity itself.

If this is the case, how should we approach the study of death in order to grasp it as revealing the ultimate structure of *Dasein*? Heidegger's answer falls back upon the results of the preliminary analysis of *Dasein* worked out in division one of *Being and Time* (par. 50). The "basic state" of *Dasein* has already been defined as "care." The structure of care, in turn, is composed of the three elements of *existence* (the "ahead-of-itself"), *thrownness* (in the "Being-already-in"), and *falling* (in the "Being alongside"). And thus, Heidegger concludes, we must determine how death reveals to us the total structure of care with its three items of existence, thrownness, and falling.

It will not be possible within the limited framework of this study to follow all the complex meanings of the expressions "existence," "thrownness," and "falling" as they are used throughout *Being and Time*. On the other hand, any attempt to frame a general definition of these terms would have to be doomed to failure. Existence, thrownness, and falling cannot be defined, since they are *existentialia*, not categories, and hence cannot be captured by some marks or features that supply the necessary and sufficient conditions needed to form a definition. In subsequent discussions we shall therefore consider existence, thrownness, and falling only as they pertain to man's encounter with death. Furthermore, both in our presentation of Heidegger's position and in the criticisms we shall formulate, we will concentrate upon death as a possibility (the "ahead-of-itself," representing the "existence" aspect of care). This choice is in full agreement with Heidegger's own view of "existence" as the primary item of care, a view which is reaffirmed at the outset of Heidegger's analysis of death (*BT*, 279).

1. *Death as existence.*—Existence is *Dasein*'s way of taking a stand on and relating to its own possibilities. Now death too is a "possibility" of mine—not in the sense that it may be possible for me not to confront death but in the sense that death is still ahead of me. But death is a very special, in fact unique, possibility. Death is the only possibility "which is one's ownmost, which is non-relational and which is not to be out-stripped [*unüber-holbare*]" (*BT*, 294). Let us consider these expressions

one by one. Death is my "ownmost" possibility, for it is I alone who can encounter my death. This, for Heidegger, is more than a trivial analytic statement. With the one and only exception of my death, everything I do and experience could have been done and experienced by someone else. Another man could have had the same career as I did; he could have had the same joys and sorrows, pleasures and pains. But I cannot imagine his having my death. Here and here only the rules of universalization break down: what my death means to me can only be realized when *I* confront my death. When, by an act of imagination, I picture the other confronting my death, this death ceases to be mine; what my death means to me is thus incommensurable with what it means, or could ever mean, to him. This is why, when I observe the other as he relates to his death, I cannot hope to achieve any understanding of what it would mean for me to face the fact of my own mortality. In the case of any other personal experience—love, marriage, political or religious commitment, etc.—I can always "put myself in the shoes of the other" and (given our shared background of practices) achieve a fairly good grasp of what it would mean for me to go through the sort of experience he is going through. Only the sense of my death cannot be gained by such reliance upon our common, his and my, background of practices. And for this reason death is a "nonrelational" possibility. Only by confronting my death do I establish myself as an individual: an individual not in the sense of being simply one particular member of a class defined by some common marks, but an individual in that deeper and more radical sense of having to go through an experience which in principle could not have appeared in the life history of any other individual. This is why death isolates me from others. No one can help me shoulder the burden of my death; no one can share it with me. To share it, another individual would have to be able to understand and to share my attitude toward my death. This no individual can do. He can understand and share all of my other experiences, but my death is a possibility that I must confront all alone. And this "ownmost" and "nonrelational" possibility is also the only possibility of mine that cannot be "outstripped." As we noted earlier, death (my ultimate end, the possibility of having no possibilities) is the final "settling of accounts"; with death, my life ceases to be what it was "before" death struck—an unfinished tale—and it becomes at last fully determined.

Two more important characteristics of death considered as a possibility are that death is both certain and, in that certainty, indefinite. For Heidegger, man's certainty of his death is of a special kind. The "evidence" for it is neither the one of an inductive generalization drawn from repeated observations of the death of others nor the sort of evidence we attribute to the propositions of a hypothetico-deductive system. Death is certain in the sense that all ways of living of a human being can be understood only as ways of living of a creature constantly involved in taking a stand, authentically or inauthentically, on the ever present possibility of its ultimate end. To describe this presence of death as being of an "indefinite" character is meant to signify that death appears as threatening man "at any moment," that it is not experienced as the natural term of a developmental process through which *Dasein* brings to fruition and then slowly uses up its own powers and dispositions. Death is absurd, for its capacity to interrupt a flourishing human life is part and parcel of what death means to us.

This last point—the indefiniteness of death as I experience it in my own case—will be of crucial importance to further considerations, and therefore we shall concentrate on it. Heidegger's position can best be grasped through a contrast with a phenomenological interpretation of death representing the exact opposite of his own. Such interpretation can be found in Max Scheler's essay "Tod und Fortleben." He too intends to articulate our personal experience of death. He too emphasizes that the sense of my death cannot be derived from any observation of the death of others. For Scheler, as for Heidegger, the sense of one's death belongs to the a priori structure of human subjectivity, and its content must be brought out through a special phenomenological inquiry. The main feature of our sense of mortality is to be found in a certain feeling of the rhythm of our life as the latter moves from birth to death. Death is lived as the term of a process through which the range of my possibilities becomes increasing reduced. Thus an adolescent's life appears to him as a wide and indefinite horizon of possibilities which he confronts with his vibrant imagination and enthusiasm. With every year that passes, the field of possibilities becomes poorer and more limited, and the role of the past increases. Routine and stagnation set in; this is why, as Scheler repeats after Windelband, the old are more inclined to a deterministic view of life while the young naturally worship freedom. Moreover, this direction of life, as it runs its course from birth to death, is not a specifically human phenomenon. For Scheler, the experience of death is essentially a biological phenomenon;

hence, consciousness of death must belong, at least to some degree, to all living beings.[1] All life—from its lowest forms to its highest—exhibits the same pattern: with aging, the powers and the possibilities of living beings diminish slowly until they are finally extinguished in death. Death is thus the fulfillment of the living process itself; a living being "accomplishes its act of dying"[2] to the extent to which death is the last step an organism takes on its path of life. Death can appear to interrupt the rhythm of life suddenly only if it is due to the operation of some external causes which destroy the organism before its life has run its inner course.[3]

What is thus phenomenologically atypical for Scheler—the indefiniteness of death—becomes essential for Heidegger. This difference was to be expected. For the author of *Being and Time*, our sense of death is most emphatically not a biological phenomenon. Thus, far from its being the case that *Dasein* perceives its death as the term of a vital process that has run its course, death appears to *Dasein* to be capable of always interrupting its life and of asserting itself against it.

2. *Death as thrownness.*—Man is "thrown" insofar as human life does not supply its own foundations, insofar, that is, as man finds himself in a situation that is not of his own choosing. One aspect of this situation is the fact of human mortality. Now thrownness is manifested in moods (*Stimmungen*). Hence there must be a mood in which the fact of human mortality is revealed to man. This mood is anxiety. In anxiety, man experiences himself as delivered to death: "Thrownness into death reveals itself to *Dasein* in a more primordial and impressive manner in . . . anxiety" (*BI*, 295; see 311).

This experience of being handed over to the power

of death is a rich and complex phenomenon which illumi-
nates the true status of man in the public world and indeed the status of that world itself. This is why anxiety
was analyzed already in division one of *Being and Time.*
Let us summarize the main points of that analysis. To begin with, anxiety is different from fear in at least two important and closely related respects. First, the object of
fear (that "in the face of which" I fear) is always a specific
danger represented by some entity within the world: a
boulder rolling down a hill, a car that has gone out of control, an impending crash on the stock exchange, etc. Second, that "about which" I fear is specific too: I fear about
this or that aspect of my situation (the robbery of my
home, the loss of my financial holdings, etc.). Now anxiety is different from fear in that both its "in the face of"
and its "about which" are nonspecific and completely indefinite. I am not anxious in the face of this or that
danger—anxiety can seize me when there is no real or
imaginary threat to confront. And I am not anxious
about this or that particular project of mine; I may be
seized by anxiety when the realization of all my goals and
purposes proceeds smoothly and gives me no reason to
worry.

Since anxiety is thus not connected with a particular
item within the world, and yet it does represent some
way of encountering our surroundings, Heidegger concludes that what causes anxiety is the world as such.
What "oppresses" us is the world itself (*BT*, 231). All of a
sudden, the world has revealed a face—its true face—
that is ordinarily concealed under the reassuring veneer
of "common sense." By the same token, since that about
which I am thus anxious while confronting the terrify-
ing, unfamiliar face of the world is nothing specific, I can

be anxious only about the mere fact that I find myself in, that I am thrown into, such a world. As Heidegger puts it, "That about which anxiety is anxious is Being-in-the-world itself" (*BT*, 232).

In order to understand this special meaning of the world (and of myself as having to live in such a world) as it emerges in anxiety, we must recall that in anxiety *Dasein* experiences its own death. The world takes on an "oppressive" meaning, for due to the anxious realization of one's own mortality, the world ceases to appear—as it did prior to an anxiety attack—as one's "home." One feels a stranger in that world; one's identity with it is broken, for one has come to realize that this world will go on even after one's death. Hence *Dasein's* feeling of alienation, of not-being-at-home (*Unheimlichkeit*) in the world.

3. *Death as falling.*—Man "falls" into the public world, for in order to conceal and cover up his own mortality he chooses to flee into the reassuring, familiar environment of common sense. Described in the categories of common sense—in the vocabulary of "The They"—my death becomes stripped of its entire threatening quality. This tranquilizing change in the status of my death is due to one single factor: when articulated in the categories of common sense, my death loses its indefiniteness and certainty and thus ceases to be truly mine. "Everybody dies," I may now say, and so "I will die too, when my time comes." But to say this is to imply that my death does not threaten me now (I still have some time left, I can put my affairs in order before death strikes, etc.). Far from its being the case that death has power over me, I (now) have power over death.

We shall not follow Heidegger any farther in his elucidation of death. We have said enough to be able to formulate our main criticism of his theory. Once again—and once again in full conformity with Heidegger's own list of priorities—we shall concentrate upon death as possibility.

Now death, we recall, is a possibility of a peculiar sort. It is, among other things, a possibility that can materialize itself at any moment. This is what Heidegger calls death's "indefiniteness"—a crucial feature without which death would lose at once its existential certainty (*BT*, 302). If we could know the date of our death, we would not have to confront it until then; thus our life would escape the sway of mortality to the precise extent to which we would be able to plan and prepare for death and thus bring it under our control. In other words, the existential certainty of my death can be nothing short of the permanent possibility of dying at every stage of my life history.

But, we shall object, why should death emerge as such an "indefinite" possibility of *Dasein*? Clearly, the connection of death with indefiniteness is not a matter of logical necessity. Here Scheler's descriptions are illuminating. For a mortal, finite being there can be only two ways of reaching its limit. Either such limited being perishes by having lived out its potential, and then death does represent that finite being's fulfillment. Or a finite being perishes before it unfolds itself, but this can be due only to the operation of some *obstacles* that interrupt that being's development. To be sure, we ought not to construe this specific finite being that Heidegger calls *Dasein* as having some fixed potential or essence to be developed. Still, the main tenet of Heidegger's doctrine is the claim that every human individual has some identity—a role defined by a certain set of possibilities—which he himself contributed to shape and which he aims to play out in his life. To say that death may at any moment prevent a man from playing out the possibilities defining his role implies that there are powers and obstacles capable of destroying him "before" he fulfills his life plan.

We submit that such powers can be found only in another man. This conclusion follows if our earlier arguments were sound. The other is the only power which is in principle capable of bringing about my annihilation. To say that I have a sense of my end as threatening me permanently, at every stage of my life, amounts to saying that I have a sense of permanent exposure to a power that can bring my end. The other is such a power.

A Heideggerian could object here, and the objection is all but formulated in *Being and Time* itself (*BT*, 305). For if the threat of death were to come at me only from an external entity—the other—then death would become a possibility that is encountered within the world. It can then become an object of manipulation and control; I can try to postpone it by taking concrete steps to defend myself against the other. But then the very indefiniteness and certainty of death disappear. Death is now, at least to some degree, within my grip; far from being helplessly at the mercy of death I now have a protective shield against it; I can plan ahead while being certain that death will not strike either now or in the immediate future. To this we make two replies.

1. It is true, of course, that the other, the embodiment of death's power over me, is outside me. He is not me; he is distinct from me. On the other hand, as my mirror copy, my alter ego, the other is myself. For this rea-

son he is not an entity subject to my power and manipulation. Against him—against myself-outside-me—I can raise no wall and build no foolproof protection. Hence the threat of death that he represents preserves all of death's certainty and indefiniteness. Death as it threatens me at the hands of the other is *indefinite*: at no moment of my life history can I be sure that the other—some other—will not succeed in destroying my defenses. To erase the indefiniteness of his mortal threat I would have to make sure that at some moment of my life the barricades I have erected against him are in principle invulnerable to his attack. But for me to gain the sense of such invulnerability, that other would have to cease being a member of my own species. For the same reason, death remains *certain*. The certainty at issue is exactly the same as in Heidegger's account. In order to attribute to the other the capacity to annihilate me, I do not need to rely upon statistical evidence drawn from newspaper descriptions of wars or murders, from the military chronicles, etc. That deadly power that I attribute to the other is bestowed upon him a priori—by the mere grasp of him as another me. In this sense, death is encountered "inside" me, i.e., independently of my observation of what goes on in the world, even though I could not be said to have this special sense of death without understanding myself as related to an other. Briefly, through the same stance by which I define myself as a human subject standing in relation to other human subjects, I also discover my own mortality in all its certainty and indefiniteness.

2. Furthermore, we can turn Heidegger's point against his own position. Far from its being the case that the indefiniteness and certainty of death could not

emerge within the life and death struggle with the other, the exact opposite seems to be true: without such (deadly) encounter, death will be stripped of both its certainty and its indefiniteness. It is well known that in his later period Heidegger came to regard his own philosophy from *Being and Time* as still rooted in the "metaphysical," technologically oriented thinking, where man is conceived as a power center bent on achieving mastery over his environment. And indeed all the detailed descriptions of *Dasein* in *Being and Time* convey that very message. The entire world is described as a structure established and organized by the projected possibilities of *Dasein*. To be sure, these possibilities are said to be limited by the not-to-be-outstripped possibility of death. To proceed now with our objection: why should they be viewed as thus limited? Why should *Dasein*'s technological power drive emerge as inherently defined by the limit of death? Why couldn't man (man as he is described in *Being and Time*) hope that the advances of technology will in due course assure his triumph over death? Of course, it is always possible to reply that such hope could concern death only when viewed as a biological phenomenon; from this, someone could infer that our experience of mortality would still be with us and would remain what it was all along. But would we still have such an experience if we could master our biological death? What would this mean: having the experience of my inevitable end while at the same time knowing full well that no such end will ever be coming?

Within our own theory this difficulty does not arise. Clearly, the mastery (actual or possible) of biological death would not change the basic facts of the situation. A life-support system that some future scientist would attach to me to extend my life span indefinitely could just as easily be destroyed by him; he would always be in a position of "pulling the plug" on me, for there is nothing I could rely upon to check his power. In its certainty and indefiniteness, death can threaten me only at the hands of the other.

If these remarks are on target, then certain implications ought to follow for our understanding of death as death reveals the two further items of care: thrownness and falling. Since the discovery of thrownness as well as the fall of man into the world of common sense both depend upon the realization of death, and since death reaches an individual *via* the threat from the other, man cannot encounter his thrownness or succumb to the tranquilizing ways of common sense without having had to sense the mortal threat of the other. And, if this is true, then at least in one respect Hobbes was more perceptive than Heidegger. For then it is indeed Hobbes's "fear of violent death" at the hand of the other—i.e., during a life and death struggle which, as Leo Strauss has shown so convincingly, represents the only test of reality for Hobbes—that sustains man's commitment to the rules of common sense and of a civilization built in conformity with these rules.[4]

The theory of human struggle is one of the central theories defended in Sartre's *Being and Nothingness*. For Sartre, the struggle of selves is essentially the struggle for one's identity. But, as I shall be arguing, Sartre has no way of accounting for the other's power to define me, and yet that is precisely what he sets out to account for. Since, in Sartre, the struggle of human selves is not construed as a life and death struggle, the other's perception of me turns out to be nothing more than a mere image, which I can always escape by my own choice of attitude toward him. The other cannot really define me; his view of me is merely a subjective perspective, which it is up to me to refuse or accept. Thus, by starting from a different point and traveling along a different route, I will be arriving at conclusions almost identical with those reached by Merleau-Ponty in his early criticism of Sartre's theory of intersubjectivity.[5] To what extent Sartre's position in the *Critique of Dialectical Reason* represents a progress over the doctrines from *Being and Nothingness* will not be a subject for concern here.[6]

What has given a solid foundation to Merleau-Ponty's criticism of Sartre is the status accorded by Sartre to the other within the context of the general treatment of the relationship between freedom and facticity in *Being and Nothingness* (*BN*, 523–31). On the one hand, the other is said to be my limit, for it is indeed my predicament to exist as constrained by his freedom (by his purposes, actions, evaluations); but, on the other hand, since nothing can exist as a limit of me without my having assumed it and determined it as such a limit, it is essentially due to my attitudes and stances that the other's freedom is seen by me as a limitation of my own. Sartre's examples lend themselves easily to this second line of reading. Sartre considers a Jew as he experiences himself in an anti-Semitic environment. The Jew is not, of course, deluded when he feels that the others have a definite and highly unfavorable image of him. They most certainly do apprehend him according to the well-known negative stereotypes and—Sartre insists—it is not up to him to deny that fact. Yet these attitudes, actions, and evaluations of anti-Semites will be of concern to him only if he allows them to concern him, through a free choice of his own attitude. If "it pleases" him (*BN*, 527) to consider anti-Semites as unworthy of his recognition and attention, if he chooses to consider them as "objects," thus explaining away their beliefs and actions as mere effects of some blind causal mechanisms, he will not find their attitudes painful or offensive. Thus a man's race—but also other related qualities such as social status, physical inferiority, or ugliness—can define him only due to his own choice, for it is up to him to let his view of himself be influenced by the view that the others have of him. The others can limit him only in the light of his autonomous choice of what is to count as limiting him. As a result, Merleau-Ponty points out, the For-itself and the For-another—I as I interpret myself, and I as I am defined by an other—are separated by a gap.[7]

However, to reduce Sartre's position to what we just said would be to oversimplify it. For even though the other cannot emerge as my limit independently of the stance that I adopt, it is also the case—incompatible as these two claims may look at first sight—that I cannot deny his quality of being my limit: "Although I have at my disposal an infinity of ways of assuming my being-for-others, *I am not able not to assume it*" (*BN*, 529). This is why, in his long chapter on "The Existence of Others," Sartre lays a great deal of stress upon the fact that what I am for the other is not a subjective image or a conception in his or my head, but a "structure of my being"— something that defines me whether I want it or not, something that permeates all my attitudes and stances. To deny that I am what the others take me to be is simply to choose a life of bad faith.

There are thus two claims involved in Sartre's position, and he is fully aware of the tension between them. On the one hand, the other is my limit. On the other hand, it is I who establish him as such a limit. What I am for the other "appears as an *a priori* limit given to my situation (since I am such for the Other) and hence as an existent which does not wait for me to give it existence; but also it appears as able to exist only in and through the free project by which I shall assume it" (*BN*, 529). The task of assuming and acknowledging my being-for-others is an "imperative," an "order" (*BN*, 529) for me; as a true order (and not my private arbitrary wish) it must be addressed to me from outside; still, precisely because it is addressed to me, it will not weigh with me unless I let it exercise its compelling power, unless, that is, I myself recognize it as a limit and a constraint upon me.

In what follows I shall argue that no such power of limiting me can be attributed to the other if the premises of Sartre's general theory of intersubjectivity are granted. What is missing in Sartre's account is the notion of the life and death struggle—the only possible encounter in which the other can emerge as limiting me.

What is Sartre's own account of the other's power to limit me? To answer this question we must go back to Sartre's systematic treatment of intersubjective relations in part three of *Being and Nothingness*. Of direct relevance to us are Sartre's analyses and descriptions in a section entitled "The Look" (*BN*, 252–302). It is, in effect, "the look of the other" which is said to impose limits upon me.

The method employed by Sartre in his elucidation of the "look" represents a blend of the Cartesian and Husserlian analyses of the *cogito* with an "ontological" study of consciousness. In other words, an analysis of purely intentional meanings is combined with a description of the being of consciousness. The analysis of meanings is Sartre's point of departure. When, after having given his first example (I am in a public park, a man passes by the benches arranged at the edge of the lawn, I look at the man) Sartre begins to focus upon the "look," the question he asks is "What do I mean when I assert that this object is a man?" (*BN*, 254). In other words, independently of all the worries about the objective grounds of my interpretation of the data (how can I tell whether what I take to be another person is not in fact a cleverly constructed robot?), I most certainly mean something when I label an element of my perceptual field a "man." And to understand what I mean by thus referring to an *x* as to a "man" I need not perform any (perceptual or other) tests and verifications. All I need is to focus on my own signifying intention. Since the question of objectivity of my belief can thus be eliminated—at least provisionally— Sartre insists that his point of departure is identical with Descartes's *cogito* (*BN*, 251, 268). This will give the method its apodictic certainty (*BN*, 251). But, on the other hand, this certainty will lead us beyond an analysis of meanings and toward a grasp of a human self's being. It will appear, as we go on, that in order even to interpret something as an "other"—in order to bestow (correctly or not) upon some item in my perceptual field the meaning "man"—it is necessary that I exist as a self already entangled in a web of relations with other selves.

Let us focus, then, upon some mundane case of my encounter with what I "mean as" (what I take to be) another man. Sartre's example has by now become a classic of contemporary philosophy: I am in a public park and I look at the man passing by. The man—he could be a robot, but I interpret him as being a man—is an object of my "look." But what I look at is a "look" too (the other is looking at the lawn, the benches, etc.) and hence my perceptual field becomes organized in a new and special way. My world is now "stolen from me"; I witness a "disintegration," a "flight" of my world, its organization around a center which "escapes" me (*BN*, 255). Prior to the appearance of the other in my perceptual field I was the latter's only point of reference: what things meant and how they were ordered and organized depended strictly upon my aims and attitudes. What has now happened is that things have acquired functions and meanings that are not bestowed upon them by my consciousness. They are organized around the consciousness of the other, and because of that I cannot bring them within my grasp. What things (this grass, these benches) mean to the other is something that is in principle beyond my reach. I can never experience and live the world as the other experiences and lives it.[8]

But, we could ask, why do I attribute such a peculiar status to the world as the latter becomes exposed to the look of the other? Sartre's answer is arrived at by a route he has already tested in his earlier accounts of negation, time, or possibility. I have this particular sense of what it means for the world (for this bench or this lawn) to be looked at by the other, for I have a sense of what it means for me to be exposed to the look of the other. When I perceive the other as he perceives items of my world, my perception is guided by a meaning borrowed from my own encounter with the other as he looks at me. "Being-seen-by-the-Other is the *truth* of seeing-the-Other" (*BN*, 257). And thus, Sartre concludes, there

must be something in my sense of being looked at by the
other that induces me to attribute to his look its peculiar
"disintegrating" quality.

Here too Sartre's descriptions are well known. In
shame and in fear I discover a total alienation of my self
caused by my experience of exposure to the look of the
other. I feel shame, for I am made into an object of the
other's appraisals and evaluations. I feel fear, for I am
now, in all my aims and projects, endangered by the freedom of the other. Briefly, the other has a view of me and
a use for me which are in principle beyond my grasp and
beyond my control. He is thus the limit of my freedom
(*BN*, 262).

Because of the emergence of the other's "look" my
consciousness acquires a nature. Suddenly, I find myself
endowed with a fixed and stable identity attributed to
me by the other: I am a "coward," or a "slob," and so on.
But again the ultimate meaning of this identity escapes
me. The latter has "a certain indetermination, a certain
unpredictability" (*BN*, 262). I can never be sure how my
actions and my words will be interpreted by the other. I
am thus "enslaved" (*BN*, 267) by the other's look in the
sense that no matter what I say and do, I cannot escape
the burden of having an identity that he has given me
and that is beyond my grasp.

The step from a mere intentionality to the underly-
ing existential experience has now been taken. When I
refer to an item in my world as to an "other," I definitely
mean something by that expression. But for me to be in a
position of employing such meanings, I must already exist as a self that is molded by the "look" of the other. The
reality of this "look" in my life is attested by the twin experiences of fear and shame in which the freedom of my

consciousness finds its insurpassable limit in the consciousness of the other.

The experience of this limit is the basis of the ensuing struggle of selves. The struggle erupts, for the consciousness gripped by fear and shame is also a negation of being. Sartre's argument can be explained as follows. To say that I am conscious of something, implies that I must be able to establish and assert my distinctness from that of which I am conscious. For example, to be conscious of this chair implies a sense of not being that chair. Without some such form of the negation of being, the very difference between consciousness and its term (that of which one is conscious) would collapse. Sartre emphasizes this point with great force, and he relies upon it in his deduction of conflict as the fundamental relation of selves (*BN*, 284). To say that I am conscious of the other implies my ability to establish myself as distinct from him, as not being him. But there is a special difficulty involved in securing this distinctness of myself from the other. Such difficulty is encountered in no other case: it is easy for me to establish myself as distinct from this house or this tree, for both of them are specific items within my perceptual field, both of them are fully accessible to my grasp. But the other is not simply an item within my perceptual field. On the contrary, as another self aware of me, the other is an "absence." He is another stream of consciousness, he is forever elusive, I can never gain a grasp of his experiences as he lives them. I therefore find nothing—nothing visible and tangible, as it were—in which to anchor the negation needed to sustain my distinctness from him. The solution that Sartre proposes to this dilemma is as follows. Since the other is an absence, my distinctness from him cannot be sustained by a "direct" negation: "my fundamental negation cannot be direct, for there is nothing on which it can be brought to bear" (*BN*, 285). However, I can negate him indirectly. Insofar as the other is another self, he is thus a source of perceptions, actions, and evaluations, some of which are directed toward me. I have a being-for-the-other—something that I am in his eyes and in his plans. Briefly, the other bestows an identity upon me. In order to establish myself as distinct from the other—as not being him—I can simply establish myself as distinct from the identity that he has attributed to me: "What I refuse is nothing but this refusal to be the Me by means of which the Other is making me an object. . . . I posit this refused Me as an alienated-Me in the same upsurge in which I wrench myself away from the Other" (*BN*, 285). In other words, if I could succeed in asserting myself as distinct from what the other takes me to be, I would have succeeded in asserting myself as distinct from him. Now, as we recall, the other attributes an identity to me through the power of his look. I must therefore disarm the look of the other, and this I can do by looking at him. If he yields to the power of my look— if, for example, he cannot sustain an eye contact—he will have been transformed into an object exposed to my evaluations and purposes. Far from being enslaved by an identity attributed to me by him, it is now I who enslave the other by an identity attributed to him by me. But the other is another me—another consciousness, another For-itself—and this is why he, in turn, must establish his distinctness from me, and hence the corresponding negation of my self by the other. Thus everything I do in pursuit of my distinctness from him, he does in pursuit of his distinctness from me. While I try to enslave him by my look, he tries to enslave me by his look. And, Sartre argues, this struggle of selves can neither cease nor be resolved by a mutual recognition.

Only now can we fully grasp the function of fear and shame in Sartre's theory of intersubjectivity. As Sartre puts it, without the "affective character of these motivations" I would have no incentive for breaking out of the fixed identity within which the other has enslaved me (*BN*, 288). I would find my slavery tolerable, perhaps even enjoyable—in fact, I would not even live it as slavery and thus the other's presence would cease to have any reality in my life—and I would shun the task of asserting myself against the other. The fact is, however, that I cannot tolerate the other's look, for I experience its power in the paralyzing, unbearable emotions of fear and shame.

But, to begin now our critical examination of Sartre's theory, why should I grant the other's look its power to enslave me? The difficulty is serious for the following reason. The recognition of the other's power to limit me by his look is extracted from me in the experience of fear and shame. Any attempt to deny this experience—as in pride—can be seen only as an act of bad faith (*BN*, 290). But, on the other hand, shame and fear are *my* emotions, and they are thus, on Sartre's own theory, dependent upon my choices and stances. It seems, then, that it is only up to me to choose the life of shame and fear: had I chosen a different attitude, I could have constituted myself as a self totally oblivious to other selves and hence not limited by them.

We shall test the strength of this objection by concentrating on Sartre's analysis of fear. It is indeed much easier to imagine someone who succeeds in making himself immune to shame than someone whose life is entirely free of fear. After all, lack of shame involves only our immunity to appraisals and evaluations of others; lack of fear may very well require total indifference to our very biological survival.

When Sartre talks about fear in the chapter on "The Existence of Others" he describes it, following up on his earlier analyses in *Esquisse d'une théorie phénoménologique des émotions*, as a "magical" solution adopted by the agent as the latter attempts to cope with specific dangers in his environment. I "succumb to fear" when I choose not to confront the danger with some real means, but to dispose of it as if by "incantation" (running away, burying my head in the sand) hoping against hope that I will make the danger disappear. Fear is thus a "cop-out"; it is a path that the agent himself chooses to enter in order to achieve definite purposes. Hence fearful conduct—and fearfulness is a way of conducting oneself in the world—cannot be made intelligible by means of a causal explanation. Sartre argues at length (*BN*, 442–45) that the difference between will and any human emotion (or passion, for that matter) is not the difference between freedom and determinism; will and emotion are simply two different strategies open to the agent as he aims at the realization of his goals. Both the goals and the strategies are always freely chosen by the agent. If, then, fear is a strategy that I choose freely, why can't I refuse to succumb to fear and thus refuse to acknowledge the other's grip upon me?

There are several ways in which this objection could be met by Sartre, and we shall consider them in a moment. But we can already rule out one such possible reply. Given the overall framework of Sartre's theory, the

other cannot be said to impose himself upon me due to
his capacity to make me fear death. Not only is my fear
of the other independent of the experience of a mortal
threat, but death as such does not even belong to the in-
timate structure of the Sartrean self (*BN*, 545). Either of
these two reasons is sufficient to show that the limit I encounter in the other—the limit which I experience in my
fear of the other—cannot be imposed upon me due to his
capacity to bring about my death. Let us examine this in
more detail.

To begin with, it cannot be said that I acknowledge
the other as my limit as soon as I realize that he has the
power to bring me face to face with my annihilation. To
say this would be to misconstrue the meaning of death
for a human self; it would be to imply that man can go on
with the business of living while taking a stand on his
own mortality. Sartre's views are here diametrically opposed to those of Heidegger. If death, with all its indefiniteness and certainty, is to be anticipated and lived by
an individual as the forthcoming "settling of accounts" in
all matters of his life, then such an individual, Sartre argues, can never be free. A free self cannot consider its
death as its own possibility (be it the Heideggerian possibility or not having any possibilities). In effect, if death
can strike "at any moment," then it is not up to me to
determine who I am when I die: even if I move ahead
quite successfully in realizing all my aims and projects,
their sudden interruption by death deprives me of the
opportunity to give my life the meaning that I intended
for it. (I was aiming to be a prolific writer, but when I die
suddenly I am only a beginner; and thus I will be remem-
bered only as a "promising young writer.") If death gives
the ultimate meaning to my life, and if I interpret death

as capable of putting an end to my endeavors at any moment, then at no stage of my life can I be said to be in a position of shaping my own identity. Far from opening, as in Heidegger, the path of "liberation" (*BT*, 311), the thought of death paralyzes a human individual, for it deprives him of any ability to determine the meaning of his life. But to give up on freedom is to deny the most fundamental quality of human consciousness. Hence death ought not to be seen as belonging to the structure of human self. This is why Sartre does not hesitate to claim that a human self could very well remain finite while at the same time becoming immortal: "human reality would remain finite even if it were immortal. . . . To be finite, in fact, is to choose oneself. . . . The very act of freedom is therefore the assumption and creation of finitude" (*BN*, 546). Briefly, mortality and finitude are not just distinct but separable; both their distinctness and their separability are due essentially to one and the same factor: human freedom. Since man is free, he is always making determinate choices—exercising his options for this rather than for that—and he is thus inherently finite. For exactly the same reason, i.e., on account of man's freedom, death cannot belong to the structure of the human self; if he is to conduct himself as a free agent, man must live as if he were not concerned about his death, as if his own death were not real to him. Nothing more is needed to show that for Sartre the other does not impose himself upon me because of his capacity of bringing me face to face with my ultimate limit in death. Whatever can be the source of the other's power to impose himself upon me, death can have nothing to do with it. I cannot acknowledge the other by acknowledging his capacity to bring about my limit in death for the very simple and en-

tirely sufficient reason that death is not lived as my limit.
If an immortal (albeit finite) self would still remain a human self and if, as Sartre says (*BN*, 382), a human self
cannot be a private, monadic ego but must be determined by its relations to other selves; if, further, we are
willing to grant Sartre that any encounter of one self
with another is tantamount to the imposition of limits
upon them, then even in a hypothetical community of immortal selves the latter would have to be limited by each
other. Yet, of course, their limits could not be a result of
any awareness of death.

In addition, it is simply not the case that for Sartre
fear of the other can be caused only by my thought that
he is capable of killing me. Other less dramatic and quite
trivial cases are entirely sufficient to make me fear the
other—as when, for example, my possibility of going out
rather than staying at home becomes suddenly a "dead
possibility" due to the other's capacity of preventing me
from leaving my apartment (*BN*, 271). It is true that the
other's threat to my possibilities may be backed up by
the threat of death, and this may even result, should I
choose to challenge him, in my actual death. But such
circumstances are in no way necessary for my experience of fear of the other.

Sartre would now say that the other can emerge as
my limit quite independently of his capacity to represent
a mortal threat to me. The other can and does limit me to
the precise extent to which he is simply another self and
is thus capable of attributing to me functions and identi-
ties which do not depend upon me. This is what I cannot
fail to realize in fear and shame, and this is what I can
deny only at the risk of committing myself to a life based
on bad faith.

However, if fear is a strategy that I freely adopt, then what is it that could ever prevent me (at least in principle) from abandoning that strategy? We speak of people who "know no fear" or who "refuse to live in fear." These ways of living seem to be perfectly possible in terms of Sartre's own theory of consciousness as total freedom. If fearful conduct expresses a free choice of the agent, it is only up to the latter to reverse that choice and to commit himself (in a total conversion perhaps) to an entirely different way of relating to his environment. Either escape from fear (especially from the fear of other) cannot be an empty pretense, an act of bad faith, but then Sartre's theory of intersubjectivity cannot be saved; or else such escape is impossible, but then Sartre's entire theory of consciousness as total freedom (and hence as being free to choose its own emotions) has to be abandoned.

To this it could be objected that my fear of the other falls into a very special category, for it represents not fear of this or that specific danger, but fear of being exposed in my entire being-in-the-world, in all of my pursuits and endeavors. Such fear would be very close to Heidegger's anxiety; it would grip me suddenly as an all-pervasive mood which it is clearly not up to me to either accept or abandon. Fear of the other, on this reading of Sartre, would thus represent not a strategy that I pursue, but the sudden realization of a threat to all my strategies—of a threat, that is, which is entirely independent of any attitude I may choose to adopt.

However, this reply could not even be formulated within Sartre's overall framework. After all, there had to be a reason that Sartre chose to talk about fear—not about anxiety—when he was describing the emotion an individual feels while encountering other individuals. More to the point, my fear of the other *is* a ("magical") strategy that I adopt (*BN*, 295). Finally, it is difficult to see how the Sartrean fear could resemble the Heideggerian anxiety without being dependent upon the sudden realization of one's own mortality. Yet, as we saw a moment ago, for Sartre my fear of the other is entirely independent of the other's capacity to bring about my death. It follows, and it must do so if we accept Sartre's theory of the total freedom of human consciousness, that it is only up to me to interpret this or that encounter with the other's "look" as an occasion for fearful conduct.

Two possibilities are now open. If, all appearances to the contrary notwithstanding, the others still exist somehow for that "fearless" individual we have just described, then fear and shame are not essential to encountering others, and it is perfectly possible to envision human selves related to each other in entirely different ways and thus entirely free of the curse of mutual "enslavement." But such a possibility is explicitly denied by Sartre (*BN*, 267), and it must be denied, since the claims Sartre is putting forward are meant to represent an ontology of intersubjective relations. If, on the other hand, one would want to reply that our individual's attitude is still built on the foundation of fear to the extent to which his very attempt at mastering fear is itself comprehensible only as a strategy of an initially fearful individual, then we would object that to say this is to solve the problem by means of an arbitrary definition. In this case, it does not matter what and how this or that individual feels when he relates to others; what does matter is our prior conception of a human self as being essentially "fearful." But to fall back upon some a priori definition of a human self is to be guilty of a mistake which Sartre detects in Heidegger's theory of intersubjectivity. According to Sartre, the reality of others must be attested, and the attestation in question is said to occur in concrete and repeated experience of fear and shame. And thus an individual who refuses to live in fear and shame—a refusal that is perfectly possible if the human self is indeed, as in Sartre, totally free—can be viewed only as an accomplished practitioner of solipsism.

We are now in a position to draw conclusions. Once again, these conclusions will follow if what we argued in our earlier chapters was on sound grounds. From our examination of Sartre we have learned that the other can never be construed as limiting me if his capacity to do so can be denied to him by a strategy which is in principle always open to me. He can emerge as my limit only if my unwillingness to acknowledge him as such a limit does not leave me free to pursue goals and strategies of my own. But in order to thus impose himself as capable of blocking all my strategies and goals, the other must emerge as a threat of my annihilation. For at the very moment that I realize him to be such a threat—at the moment that he brings me face to face with the prospect of my death—I am no longer in a position where I can freely pursue my strategies and goals while continuing to ignore him. To refuse to acknowledge him *then* would amount to my inviting the collapse of all my strategies and goals. Thus the other "enslaves" me, not by his capacity to subsume me under labels that are not to my liking but by his threat to my very life. It is on this level— not on the level of images and representations formed by his mere "look"—that I experience his reality, and it is on this level that I discover myself as a limited self.

One more point needs to be made in this connection. Since it is impossible to defend the Sartrean view of the other as the limit of a human self while at the same time removing death from that self's fundamental structure, Sartre's criticism of Heidegger could not have been on sound grounds: death and human finitude are inseparable.[10]

Chapter 5

Hegel on the Life and Death Struggle

ALEXANDRE Kojève has presented contemporary readers with an interpretation of Hegel built around the notion of the life and death struggle.[1] One need not agree fully with Kojève to recognize that the idea of the struggle of selves is called upon by Hegel to illuminate such crucial notions as consciousness and self-consciousness. At different stages of his philosophical career Hegel kept making two points: self-consciousness is the truth of consciousness;[2] mutual recognition of selves—a result of their life and death struggle—is the truth of self-consciousness.[3] Hegel's talk about "truth" here has a special, strictly Hegelian meaning. Consciousness, self-consciousness, recognition—these are all important stages of the "subjective mind." For Hegel the "higher" stage is always the "truth" of the "lower." This position involves two claims. First, the full potential of the lower stage can be realized only within the framework supplied by the higher stage. Second, the lower stage is in fact an aspect (a "moment," to use the Hegelian terminology) of the higher one. These two rules guide Hegel in his deduction of the stages of mind and of mind's categories. For example, the identity-and-difference of the categories of Being and Nothing finds its realization in the immediately following category of Becoming. Furthermore, Being and Nothing do not exist apart from Becoming; they are simply aspects of the latter; Becoming is the vanishing of Being into Nothing (ceasing-to-be) and the change from Nothing to Being (coming-to-be). Similarly, consciousness is realized in self-consciousness; self-consciousness, in turn, is realized in a plurality of human selves as they grant each other recognition.

But how are we to understand these claims? And what light do they shed upon Hegel's view of the life and death struggle? Perhaps the clearest exposition of what Hegel means by "consciousness" and "self-consciousness" can be found in the third volume of the *Encyclopedia*, although the general pattern of the theory had been set already in the Jena system. This theory is deepened and treated at length in both the *Phenomenology of Mind* and the monumental *Science of Logic*.

By "consciousness," Hegel understands a form of experience in which we tend to draw a sharp boundary line between our own cognitions and beliefs and the external reality. At this stage of experience, reality is interpreted as fully independent of our mental life, and the object of knowledge reigns supreme as the only standard for assessing the value of our cognitive claims. Any contribution of the knowing self is discarded at once as a source of error and distortion. The truth of propositions is viewed as their correspondence with external reality—with qualities and relations of things as they exist independently of human cognitive powers. This does not mean that man can ever succeed in thus purifying knowledge from his own assumptions. Even the most elementary stage of consciousness, the stage of sense-certainty, turns out to be dependent upon such assumptions, since the grasp of sensible particulars (of this tree, of this house) is impossible without reliance upon human language and its rules. But a merely "conscious" self refuses repeatedly, until the very end of consciousness's last stage in "understanding," to recognize this dependence of knowledge upon man's cognitive powers. Confronted with a mode of cognition in which his own assumptions contribute to shape cognitive claims, man persists in refusing to view them as pieces of genuine knowledge. His hope is then to construct a more sophisticated way of grasping things and hence to succeed in discovering them as they are independent of his own beliefs and assumptions about them. Self-consciousness emerges when this hope is finally abandoned and when the self, in a typically idealistic fashion, begins to view reality as in some sense dependent upon mind. At the stage of consciousness the self interpreted itself as passive and contemplative; its aim was to adjust its cognitions to what is "out there," as it were, untainted by any imprint of human mind. The stage of self-consciousness is the exact opposite of that former contemplative and passive attitude. In self-consciousness, reality ceases to be viewed as something independent of the self. The world is now interpreted as the extension of the self, and the latter's aim is to confirm that view by actively destroying any

remnants of reality's independence. At the stage of self-
consciousness man is thus bent on demonstrating that
reality will not resist him, that it has no power over him.
An individual self-consciousness will pursue this aim by
unleashing crude appetites and desires against reality;
it is this aim, Hegel will argue, that will guide self-
consciousness in its search for recognition by another
self-consciousness.

Throughout Hegel's analysis of consciousness and
self-consciousness there are references to the dialectics
of the "I" and its "other" (*das Andere*). The stage of consciousness emerges when the I is capable of breaking all
the ties binding it to its "other." Now the "other" of the
human self is the entire content found in man's immediate impulses, feelings, or sensations (i.e., in his body)
and in his external environment. To emerge as a conscious self—as the pure I—the self must thus set itself
apart from its own body and from its external environment. Its body appears now as only one particular item
in the furniture of the objective world instead of being
viewed (as it still was at the essentially preconscious
stages of the "soul") as intimately connected with the life
of mind. Only now does the I emerge as an objective I,
i.e., as capable of establishing firm boundaries between
itself and the world.

To an I merely conscious of objective reality the
"other" appears as entirely independent. Here lies the
difference between the objective "I" as it emerges in consciousness and the same objective "I" establishing itself
as self-consciousness. "The pure abstract freedom of
mind lets go from it its specific qualities—the soul's natural life—to an equal freedom as an independent *object*. It
is of this latter, as external to it that the *ego* is in the first

instance aware (conscious), and as such it is Consciousness" (*Enc.* IV, par. 413). In self-consciousness, the relationship of the objective "I" and its other is reversed. To be sure, since consciousness is incorporated into self-consciousness as an aspect of the latter (*PhM*, 220), the I's other cannot return to the status it enjoyed at the preconscious stages of mind. We are still talking about the objective "I," not about the "soul" (*Seele*) which is in principle unable to separate itself from reality. Reality—the self's other—remains set over against the self: the self does not confuse the object with its own feelings and sensations. But that reality is now seen as dependent upon the powers of the objective (the pure) I. At the present stage (of self-consciousness) the object is interpreted as being the representation of such a pure I. "The object is my idea: I am aware of the object as mine; and thus in it I am aware of me" (*Enc.* III, par. 424).

In self-consciousness, then, the object is an idea, a representation of the "I." This account gives us the material we need to understand Hegel's claim that self-consciousness is the "truth" of consciousness; the former realizes the latter. Hegel gives the following reason for this dependence of consciousness upon self-consciousness in the *Science of Logic*: "Consciousness, even as such, contains in principle the determination of being-for-self [of self-consciousness] in that it *represents* to itself an object which it senses, or intuits, and so forth; that is, it has *within it* the content of the object, which in this manner has an 'ideal' being . . ." (*SL*, 158). This statement summarizes well the main thrust of Hegel's more detailed expositions of the argument as it occurs, for example, at the end of the chapter on "Understanding" in the *Phenomenology of Mind*. What he starts with is consciousness's ability to form a representation of the object. Consciousness, let us repeat, is a stage of mind where mind is not immersed in its feelings, inclinations, and sensations; in consciousness, mind is related to an independent object by forming an idea, a conception of it. Furthermore, the conception itself is seen not as a product of the self's own fantasies and wishes but as matching the object. Hegel now suggests—these are the very words he uses in the passage we have just quoted—that the emergence, in mind, of the representation of the object signifies that the latter has in fact only an "ideal being" "within" the mind. The step from consciousness to self-consciousness has now been taken. It represents a radicalization of Kantian idealism. In order to form a representation of the object, mind must impose its own laws upon reality, for as Kant proved, the lawful character of what counts as the object of knowledge is impossible to explain other than by reference to mind's own cognitive powers. When followed to its ultimate conclusions, this thought leaves no room for any independence of the object from the self. The notion of some allegedly independent "things in themselves" is in fact, Hegel argues, a self-contradictory notion (*PhM*, 192). For, on the one hand, something of which we can form no conception at all has no meaning to us; on the other hand, were we to succeed in forming a conception of "things in themselves," they would become at once relative to our own modes of conceiving and representing them. To conclude: self-consciousness is the "truth" of consciousness, for the latter's ability to form conceptions and representations of objects implies that the objects in question must be viewed as being dependent upon the self's own powers. In other words, the self's capacity to form representa-

tions of objects can be realized only by a self that is actively shaping the objects thus represented; mind can
represent only what it itself has constructed.

Hegel's next step, the demonstration of self-consciousness's dependence upon recognition, will emerge
fully only after we have explained the meaning of the recognition itself. At the present stage we can at best convey
the general sense of Hegel's move. Self-consciousness
finds its truth in the recognition of selves by each other
because the self gains a conception of itself as a fully developed objective I (the stage of self-consciousness) only
by achieving recognition. When the self enters the relations of recognition with other selves, reality ceases to
appear as an alien and independent realm which con-
strains the self's cognitive and practical powers. Thus
what self-consciousness aims at from the beginning becomes fulfilled and realized in a community of selves
granting each other recognition. We must try to make
clear the role played by recognition, especially since Hegel's view of the life and death struggle—the main subject of our interest—is inextricably woven with his idea
of recognition.

Here as elsewhere, the self's attitude is made up of
two claims which appear at first incompatible. On the
one hand, I am bent on excluding another self; I cannot
tolerate its presence as an independent self-consciousness, for my own claim to be such self-consciousness
seems to be incompatible with the independence of anything outside me. On the other hand, I need the other,
and I need him precisely as a free and independent self,
for only a free and independent self could grant me a recognition which would not be worthless. "For us"—this is
how Hegel refers to the point of view of the philosopher

as he considers things from the ultimate perspective of Absolute Knowledge—these two impulses of the self searching for recognition must and can be reconciled. But this truth has not yet dawned upon the self in question. Following blindly and unthinkingly its first impulse, the self will set out to exclude the other by simply killing him or (at best) by enslaving him. Only after the discovery of the unfruitfulness of the path of exclusion will the self be ready to acknowledge its need for another self and (given proper conditions) to grant the latter recognition. Finally, let us note that, for the reasons we will spell out later, both impulses can be fulfilled only through a life and death struggle and both, involving as they do aims of man's spiritual self, are not of a merely biological nature. Both represent man's attempts to act out and confirm a certain conception of himself. Thus the life and death struggle is from the very beginning a "battle for ideas." It remains, to be sure, a genuine life and death struggle, but the combatants are engaged in it for the sake of testing an image they have of themselves and of each other. This point will be of crucial importance to us when we begin to examine Hegel's theory critically.

We shall now discuss in more detail the two impulses motivating an individual to enter the life and death struggle.

The need to exclude the other.—The most extensive treatment of the need to exclude the other can be found in the Jena system.[4] What Hegel has to say about it in his later writings (*PhM*, 231) represents a compressed version of his suggestive analyses from the Jena period. Hegel's point of departure is simple enough. Self-consciousness—in the Jena system Hegel prefers to talk about a "totality of consciousness" (*Totalität des Be-*

wusstseins) and hence also about the struggle of two such totalities (*Der Kampf zweier Totalitäten*, as the relevant fragment is entitled)—is first of all an *individual* self. Now these two qualities of the self—being a self-consciousness and being an individual—are at the root of the ensuing life and death struggle. As an individual, the self finds itself opposed to other individuals. This, for Hegel, is a matter of conceptual necessity which applies to individuals of any kind, not only to human selves (*SL*, 167–69). However, my acknowledgement of other selves' reality would be incompatible with my self's certainty of being a totality, i.e., with my self's certainty of being able to enclose all of reality within its boundaries. The presence of another self is a challenge to that certainty, an act of defiance by external reality. Something has emerged in that reality—another self—which refuses to submit to my self's authority and power. My self's claim to be a genuine totality is thus badly shaken. In order to beat down that challenge of reality my self has no alternative but to set out to destroy the challenger: the other self. Thus my self aims at the death of the other self. But in the ensuing life and death struggle I cannot remain attached to my own life. For were this to be the case, my entire initial conception of myself as a totality would have been an illusion to begin with, since I would not even have been able to master my own natural (merely biological) self. The enemy is outside me as another self, but he is also inside me as my own blind attachment to life. Thus in aiming at the death of the other I must also face and endure the thought of my own death.[5] This is why the assertion of the self as an individual totality is achieved through the experience of the "nothingness of death" (*Nichts des Todes*).[6]

The need to acknowledge the other.—In the "Philosophische Propädeutik," Hegel points out that the self's first impulse toward the other, the impulse to assert oneself at the price of killing or enslaving the other, is only a form of the "negative freedom."[7] He notes, in the same passage, that such freedom "does not correspond to the notion of freedom," and he points out that what is now required is the self's reconciliation with the other self, the acknowledgement of the second self by the first self. In effect, the other's independence is not at all a challenge to my own self-conception. As we shall see in a moment, by recognizing the other I confirm myself as self-consciousness.

It is highly significant and illuminating that Hegel chooses to speak in this context about the "negative freedom" embodied in one's impulsive drive to deny the other any independent status. The concept of negative freedom has a fairly precise meaning in Hegel's philosophy, and it is also a concept of great importance. An individual committed to a merely negative view of freedom is someone who has decided to act with total disregard for the actions' natural and social setting.[8] Such an agent will conduct himself as if his needs and inclinations, his social and historical position, simply don't matter to him. He may commit himself to the pursuit of some utopian ideals, or else he may set out to prove his total independence from reality by destroying everything, including even his own life. (Hegel would have found perfect examples of these attitudes in Dostoevsky's Stavrogin and Kirilov.) Needless to say, Hegel analyzes the idea of negative freedom only to debunk its mythology. This is the purpose of his painstaking search for the "hypocrisies" implied by the "moral" (Kantian and Fichtean) view of the world (*PhM*, 628–41). This too, is at the root of his diagnosis of Stoicism and Scepticism (*PhM*, 243–51). Last but not least, in his philosophy of history and of state, Hegel shows time and again how a truly free activity takes place only when the agent sets himself within his natural and social situation.

In all these cases Hegel's dialectic pursues one and the same path. A self committed to a merely negative form of freedom sets out to exclude its "other"—to liberate itself from the constraints of needs, inclinations, laws, institutions and so on, briefly from any dependence upon reality. But since the self's drive to achieve such total autonomy leads inevitably to a failure—in fact, to the exact opposite of what the self aimed at, i.e., to a form of bondage—the self must acknowledge its "other" and make it part and parcel of its own life.

The "other" is a generic term which covers also that specific area of external reality encountered as another man. Here too the self must take the step from negative to positive freedom. The self's search for autonomy through total exclusion of other selves is counterproductive since the autonomy searched for is in fact tied up with the recognition of the autonomy of other selves. In effect, I am not only an individual self-consciousness, but I am also a self which is, and strives to be, a universal, communal self-consciousness. I can thus become a fully human self, a self capable of realizing and displaying its specifically human powers, only by relating to (and thus acknowledging the independence of) a human environment. The other must become an object of my recognition.

The idea of recognition is practically inexhaustible in its richness and complexity. What is important to our concerns in this study is the role of recognition in the emergence of mind as self-consciousness, i.e., as a fully developed objective agent and knower. Happily, this interest of ours coincides with the main purpose that Hegel himself had in mind while focusing on recognition, especially in the celebrated chapter on "Lordship and Bondage" in the *Phenomenology of Mind*. We have already described the main thrust of Hegel's argument. We shall now present this argument in a more detailed way.

In order to establish himself as an objective knower and agent, an individual must be capable of showing his freedom and independence from impulses, inclinations, desires, and so on—briefly, from everything that could distort the impartiality and autonomy of his judgment. The litmus test of this ability lies in his readiness to risk his life. By undertaking such a risk he endangers the most powerful of his desires, the desire to stay alive, and thereby proves that no desire can have power over him. But, and this is where the role of recognition becomes crucial, that risk of life taken for the sake of proving one's independence from all impulses and desires can have worth only if confirmed and validated by another individual who is a competent judge. No matter how much courage I might display in confronting some mortal danger, I could never tell, by myself, whether my courage is motivated by this or that desire (be it even the desire to "live dangerously," to "get my thrills" that way, etc.) as opposed to the need to prove my ability to rise above all desires. Now, to be a competent judge of my ability to risk my life (or of anything else, for that matter) the other must expose his life to mortal danger, and he too must do so not out of this or that desire but out of his need to assert himself as capable of rising above his desires. Only thus can he prove that his judgment is not distorted by his impulses and desires. He too cannot prove it all alone, since his conception of himself is in turn in need of validation by another self. Hence, when we engage each other in a life and death struggle while aiming at proving our independence from the instinct of self-preservation, our action is a "double entente" (*PhM*, 231). While proving myself I also prove the other and I cannot prove myself without allowing the other to successfully prove himself; conversely, while proving his freedom and independence from impulse, he in turn must entice me to prove myself, since his self-image cannot be validated by someone who shuns the life and death struggle, by someone who is enslaved by fear of death. A recognition extracted from a cowardly and thus unfree self would be worthless. Hegel's somewhat mysterious claim that I can become "aware of me as myself in another individual"[9] becomes less puzzling now. Plato had already defined thinking as a dialogue with oneself.[10] In Plato's view, thinking is a "dialogue" to the extent to which it involves a constant challenge to one's assumptions and beliefs; thinking is thus an argument conducted with and against oneself.[11] Now what Hegel wants to say is that such inner dialogue with oneself can be carried on only if the self can look at itself from the perspective of another self. I am not objective—genuinely self-critical towards myself—unless I can examine my beliefs and assumptions with exactly the same severity with which another self would examine them. Only then do I become truly impartial. I thus internalize the point of view of the other; I am related to him even while carrying on a dialogue with myself. In Hegel's terms: my relation to myself is mediated by the other. The other is myself, for my identification with him allows me to rise to the level of a reflective, thinking attitude toward myself. And this attitude is the essential component of self-consciousness.

We can now see with more clarity the importance of the life and death struggle for achievement of mutual recognition. To be a partner in a dialogue with me, the other cannot be a mere echo. Since I must be prepared to test my beliefs by exposing them to an examination conducted from his point of view, I must treat his speech as capable of embodying genuine reasons. I cannot discard the worth of the other's utterances by explaining them away as a mere camouflage of his particular interests and desires. I must assume that he "speaks freely," i.e., that he defends a point of view independent of any (conscious or unconscious) prudential concerns. But there is only one test through which the other is capable of convincing me that he is worthy of recognition as such a genuinely free speaker, and that is the attitude displayed by him in the life and death struggle. Nothing short of that test will do. Already in his Jena lectures Hegel has considered and rejected the possibility that the other could emerge as worthy of my recognition merely due to his ability to communicate with me verbally and to use his speech in order to induce me—with promises, assurances, pleas and so on—to grant him that recognition.[12] The other's claim to be considered as my partner in a dialogue will not become real (*wirklich*) unless he proceeds to prove his freedom from crude impulses by forgoing all prudential considerations in a life and death battle with me. Until I encounter him as an unbending combatant he has no claim upon me; I can have pity or contempt for him, but I cannot grant him recognition. All of this applies equally to the genuineness of his moral pronouncements. Should he prove himself unable to stand up to me in a life and death struggle, he will not deserve to be taken seriously as a moral evaluator. Since his overpowering interest in staying alive prevents him from considering any morality that may endanger that interest, he cannot rise to the level of a genuine moral discourse; his evaluations are all stained by his slavish attachment to life. A reading of Bruno Snell's master-piece *Discovery of the Mind* will quickly convince us how close Hegel's position is to the Greek (and indeed Socra-tic) view of *areté*.[13]

The major weakness of Hegel's theory of the life and death struggle (perhaps the word "weakness" is too gen-eral to convey the specific nature of the difficulty) is a genuine internal contradiction in the theory. To bring out this contradiction we must pay close attention to the wording Hegel himself has chosen to express his views. On the one hand, (1) the selves as they exist prior to the struggle for recognition are said to be "modes of con-sciousness that have not risen above the bare level of life."[14] The selves do rise above the level of life only through the combat in which the participants risk their lives for the sake of freedom. Furthermore, Hegel con-trasts human consciousness with a merely organic being: "That which is confined to a life of nature is unable of it-self to go beyond its immediate existence; but by some-thing other than itself it is forced beyond that; and to be thus wrenched out of its setting is its death."[15] But, on the other hand, (2) to expose oneself to the risk of death (even if only in response to the challenge of the other) in order to establish oneself as free of the slavish attach-ment to life *is* to go beyond one's "immediate existence." Hence, Hegel's first claim is clearly incompatible with the second. Hegel, it seems, is attributing to a merely natural human self certain powers and aspirations which can only be attributed to man's spiritual self.

This difficulty, which we shall return to in a moment, is by no means limited to Hegel's view of the life and death struggle. His interpretation of human desire or appetite (*Begierde*) is an even more glaring example of the contradiction in question. On the one hand, as a being of *Begierde*, man is said to act as a mere being of nature; here "appetite has as yet no further determination than that of impulse—so far as this is not determined by thought" (*Enc. III*, par. 426). This merely appetitive drive is something that man shares with all living creatures. (*Enc. III*, par. 426). The self active in *Begierde* is man's natural self, undisciplined and unconstrained by thinking, incapable even of postponing gratification. Whatever "reality" such a self encounters, it encounters it only as destined for immediate consumption. (We will have to wait for the emergence of service and labor to see the self acquire the ability to postpone the gratifications of its desires.) And yet, on the other hand, Hegel attributes to the merely natural self of *Begierde* sophisticated powers and capacities which, according to his own view, characterize man's spiritual self. We should recall here Jean Hyppolite's illuminating point: desire, for Hegel, is intentional, it has a meaning, and, if only for that reason, it can never be viewed as an attitude of a merely natural self.[16] The evidence supporting this way of reading Hegel's theory of desire is not difficult to supply. In the *Phenomenology of Mind*, Hegel consistently describes *Begierde* as a drive to act out and confirm a conception the agent has of himself and of the world (*PhM*, 220). The agent interprets the world as his own reflection, but the apparent independence of objects challenges that self-conception, and so he sets out to prove his power over objects by making them fall under the sway of his unrestrained impulses and appetitions. Far from being an attitude of a merely natural self, *Begierde* turns out to be a response to a truly conceptual tension that must be resolved if the agent's idea of himself is to be validated. *Begierde*, here, expresses an aspiration of man's spiritual self.

The contradiction we have found in Hegel's position can now be put in terms even more menacing to the coherence of his entire theory of the struggle for recognition. Moreover, these are the very same terms that Hegel himself used while so ably and eloquently criticizing the theories of social contract. In effect, a careful reading of Hegel's own texts will soon reveal that the qualities attributed by him to man's natural (i.e., "pre-social") self can be found only in a self standing in, and hence shaped by, specifically social relations.

According to Hegel, the struggle for recognition occurs in the state of nature (*Enc.* III, Par. 432), and it creates the foundation of the entire social order, "the commencement of the political union," as Hegel puts it (*Enc.* III, par. 433). Furthermore, human individuals as they exist prior to the struggle for recognition are themselves merely natural beings; Hegel has said this much in a passage we have quoted earlier (*PhM*, 231), and he elaborates on the idea in several other places. For example, in his perhaps most widely read work, *Lectures on the Philosophy of History*, Hegel emphatically denies the existence of freedom in the state of nature, and he then goes on to describe that state as the realm of "untamed natural impulses, of inhuman deeds and emotions." What is more important, even the desire for freedom is absent from the state of nature, since "a limitation by society and the state . . . is part of the process through which is first produced the consciousness of and the desire for freedom in its true, that is, rational and ideal form."[17] By freedom in its "rational and ideal form" Hegel means both freedom *from* the tyranny of impulse and freedom *under* the law.[18] Now, it is true that individuals who enter the struggle for recognition do not yet aim at the realization of freedom under the law. Still, they do aim at the liberation from the subjection to their own impulses. This is the main purpose, indeed the only purpose, of a struggle in which individuals are called upon to free themselves from the most powerful of all impulses, the impulse to persist in being. But if such is the case, then men as they exist in the state of nature do have a conception of and a desire for freedom from impulse. Yet to say this, Hegel himself was warning us, would be to illegitimately extrapolate man's social qualities back into the state of nature. Even a sympathetic and brilliant commentator will not be able to resolve this contradiction in Hegel's position.[19]

But couldn't we avoid the contradiction in question by denying the very assumptions that led to it? Our purpose is the same as Hegel's: to account for the emergence of the objective self by relying upon the notion of the life and death struggle. But do we really need to construe the life and death struggle as the Hegelian battle for ideas—an impossible contest in which the combatants who confront each other in the state of nature would be called upon to risk their lives for the (socially conditioned) ideals of freedom and independence? It seems not. In effect, we have been arguing all along that objective selves emerge from a struggle where the combatants are not at all interested in risking their lives for the sake of ideals. The conception of objective reality is imposed upon the combatants as they are forced to face the prospect of their death; they need not be viewed as deliberately seeking out the mortal danger of the life and death struggle in order to live up to an ideal of freedom. Interestingly enough, Hegel himself sometimes seems to be thinking along these lines.

Let us consider the Hegelian slave. He is the man who didn't endure the thought of the "nothingness of death"; he is the man who preferred life and security to freedom and dignity; he is the man whose will succumbed to impulse and who therefore chose to surrender to his adversary. He has won the prize and paid the price: he is alive, but he is not free. His will reflects the will of the master; his being-for-self (*Fürsichsein*) is an alien being-for-self, since his actions are governed by the self of the master.[20] But, through a curious reversal of roles, it is the slave—not the master—who will emerge as capable of grasping objective reality. The master, intoxicated with his power and superiority, begins to view his own desires as the only measure of reality. Considering himself a superior being he is convinced that the world's only raison d'être is to gratify his desires. And he has the means to implement that conviction: by making the slaves work for him he assures the immediate gratification of his desires and wishes. Hence the last trace of objective reality disappears quickly from the master's experience: he meets no insurmountable obstacles and no immovable objects; whatever "objects" he is surrounded by are considered to be, and soon become in fact, mere articles of his private enjoyment. In contrast, the slave develops a conception of reality, and he is forced to live up to it. In service, the slave represses and postpones his own desires in order to minister to the desires of the master. In labor, the slave adopts an objective, thinking attitude toward nature, for in order to transform nature in conformity with his master's wishes he must rely more and more upon knowledge of nature; he thus rises to the view of the world that is not determined by his personal biases and prejudices; he becomes educated to reality. Hegel adds that both service and labor must be seen as imposed upon the slave through his fear of death at the hands of the master. If the slave served and worked out of his own desire, he could never rise to grasp objective reality; his would be "a merely vain and futile mind of his own" (*PhM*, 240). Briefly, he would still be realizing his peculiar preferences and goals instead of submitting to something—to the master's will—that is radically distinct from him and that therefore gives him the notion of a fully independent external reality. To be sure, the slave is in the grip of his desire to stay alive. But, it now turns out that this desire is not an obstacle to the slave's ability to gain a grasp of objective reality. Hegel now begins to pursue an entirely different approach to the problem. Because of the fear of death instilled in his breast by the master, the slave develops the objective, detached attitude toward his own personal self even while he remains unable to risk his life for the sake of freedom. His fear of death is the "sovereign master" (*PhM*, 237) to him, for in fearing death the slave grasps his own finitude, and hence also the vanity of all his personal ambitions, passions, and strivings. He thus gains an impersonal perspective upon life, he is now ready to live the life of wisdom. Thus, while the initially "fearless" master sinks deeper and deeper into the realm of his private desires, the "fearful" slave asserts himself more and more as a truly objective self. It is true that he once desired to be free. But this desire plays no part in the slave's emergence as an objective self. He becomes such a self not on account of his ability to risk life for ideal but because he is forced to face the prospect of his death at the hands of another man.

Notes

PREFACE
1. L. Strauss, *The Political Philosophy of Hobbes*, chap. 2.
2. P. Hoffman, *The Anatomy of Idealism: Passivity and Activity in Kant, Hegel, and Marx*.

CHAPTER 1
1. T. Hobbes, *Leviathan*, p. 184.

CHAPTER 2
1. Plato, *Parmenides*, 133b–35c.
2. R. Descartes, *Meditations on First Philosophy*, pp. 26–27.

CHAPTER 3
1. I. Kant, "Critique of Practical Reason," in *Critique of Practical Reason and Other Writings in Moral Philosophy*, p. 202.

2. P. Hoffman, "The Sensible and the Supersensible in Hegel's Theory of Human Action." See also Hoffman, *The Anatomy of Idealism*, chap. 3.
3. "The determination of abstractly universal individuality essentially belonging to the 'I' constitutes its being": G. W. F. Hegel, *Hegel's Philosophy of Nature, Part Two of the Encyclopaedia of the Philosophical Sciences*, par. 413.
4. G. W. F. Hegel, *Hegel's Philosophy of Right*, Introduction, par. 5.
5. Ibid.
6. Ibid., par. 6.
7. E. Fleischmann, *La Philosophie politique de Hegel*, p. 31.
8. S. Kierkegaard, *Fear and Trembling and the Sickness unto Death*, p. 168.
9. Ibid., p. 169.
10. Ibid., pp. 148–49.
11. It could be argued that our remark misses the point of Heidegger's view of guilt and conscience since for Heidegger (*BT*, p. 353) the "voice of conscience" (*Ruf des Gewissens*) summons the agent to take up the responsibility for his *whole* life, i.e., precisely for his entire self as it stretches from birth to death. But there is an ambiguity here. Either it is the case that I accept my entire mortal self due to a prior and independent decision to assume my guilt and responsibility—but then I can pursue the strategy of refusal, since the avoidance of my responsibility does not spell the end of all my strategies. Or else, on the contrary, I accept my guilt only because I have already come to terms with my mortality; in this case it would be true that, having encountered my limit, I cannot refrain from accepting my entire self (except by a flight into the inauthenticity of *Das Man*), but then it would also be true that the power making me accept my entire self is not conscience but death itself. With this we fully concur, but we continue to hold that the sense of my mortality reaches me via the threat of the other. Thus the acceptance of my entire (i.e., also factical) self depends upon my involve-

ment in a life and death struggle with the other. This is precisely the view I shall advance in the remaining section of this chapter.

CHAPTER 4

1. M. Scheler, "Tod und Fortleben," p. 17.
2. Scheler quotes Goethe as having said "dass der Tod niemals als blosses Überwaltigwerden vorgestellt werden könne, dass es zum Wesen des Todes gehöre, dass das Lebewesen selbst den actus des Sterbens vollziehe" (ibid., p. 24).
3. Ibid., p. 23.
4. See Strauss, *Hobbes*, chap. 2.
5. M. Merleau-Ponty, *Phenomenology of Perception*, pp. 448–49.
6. On this question, see H. L. Dreyfus and P. Hoffman, "Sartre's Changed Conception of Consciousness: From Lucidity to Opacity," pp. 229–45.
7. M. Merleau-Ponty, *Sense and Non-Sense*, p. 73.
8. "This green turns towards the Other a face which escapes me. I apprehend the relation of the green to the Other as an objective relation, but I cannot apprehend the green *as* it appears to the Other" (*BN*, p. 255).
9. "The For-itself is not being, for it makes itself explicitly for-itself as not being being. It is consciousness of—as the internal negation of—. The structure at the basis of intentionality and of selfness is the negation, which is the *internal* negation of the For-itself to the thing. The For-itself constitutes itself outside in terms of the thing as the negation of that thing" (*BN*, p. 123).
10. It is difficult to avoid the impression that Sartre has missed Heidegger's point. For Heidegger, the "anticipatory resoluteness" (courage-and-responsibility in the face of one's death) is in fact closely tied up with the awareness of death's indefiniteness. To be courageous and responsible for my entire life while facing my death does not mean that I have to "wait for" or "expect" (these are Sartre's

expressions) death to strike at any moment; it means only
that all my expectations and projects must be undertaken
with a lucid awareness of their precariousness. I must be
aware that the meaning I try to give to my life is at the
mercy of the meaningless, and yet I must persist in trying
to give my life that meaning.

CHAPTER 5

1. Alexandre Kojève, *Introduction à la lecture de Hegel.*
2. *PhM*, pp. 211–12; *Enc. III*, par. 424.
3. *PhM*, pp. 226–27, 229; see also G. W. F. Hegel, "Nürnberger Schriften, Bewusstseinslehre und Logik 1808/
   1809," p. 21, par. 19.
4. G. W. F. Hegel, "Jenenser Realphilosophie, Philosophie
   des Geistes," pp. 226–30.
5. Ibid., pp. 228–29.
6. Ibid., p. 229.
7. G. W. F. Hegel, "Philosophiche Propädeutik," par. 35.
8. Hegel, *Hegel's Philosophy of Right*, Introduction, par. 5.
9. *Enc. III*, par. 431; see also "Philosophische Propädeutik,"
   par. 30.
10. Plato, *Theaetetus* 189e; *Sophist* 263e.
11. Plato, *Theaetetus* 189e.
12. "Jenenser Realphilosophie," p. 227.
13. Bruno Snell, *The Discovery of the Mind*, pp. 186–87.
14. *PhM*, p. 231: "in das *Sein* des Lebens . . . versenkte Be-
    wusstsein(e)," in *Die Phänomenologie des Geistes*, p. 143.
15. *PhM*, p. 138: "Was auf ein natürliches Leben beschränkt
    ist, vermag durch sich selbst nicht über sein unmit-
    telbares Dasein hinausgetrieben; aber es wird durch ein
    anderes darüber hinausgetrieben, und dies Hinausgeris-
    sen werden ist sein Tod" (ibid., p. 69).
16. Jean Hyppolite, *Genesis and Structure of Hegel's "Phe-
    nomenology of Spirit*," p. 157.
17. *Reason in History*, p. 54.
18. See an interesting and clear exposition by R. L. Schacht,
    "Hegel on Freedom," pp. 289–328.

19. This is what Charles Taylor attempts to do by suggesting that "men at a raw and undeveloped stage of history try to wrest recognition from one another without reciprocating," (*Hegel*, p. 153). But if History, in contrast with Nature, involves, by its very essence, change towards higher and better forms of social order (*Reason and History*, pp. 68–69); if, further, the state is the "medium of historical change" (ibid., p. 61); and if the state can be established only on the basis of a *prior* struggle for recognition (*Enc. III*, par. 433), then it is difficult to avoid the conclusion that Taylor's "raw and undeveloped stage of history" (which Taylor sees as the setting of the struggle for recognition) is in fact identical with the state of nature. This conclusion is in full conformity with Hegel's view about where the struggle for recognition takes place: "in the natural state, where men exist as simple, separate individuals . . ." (*Enc. III*, par. 432). And then the difficulty we have been wrestling with all along reappears: the struggle for recognition is said to take place in the state of nature, but the combatants are endowed with capacities and aspirations which could have emerged only in society.

20. *Nürnberger Schriften, Bewusstseinslehre und Logik 1808/1809*, par. 27.

References

Descartes, R. *Meditations on First Philosophy*. Indianapolis: Bobbs-Merrill Company, 1960.

Dreyfus, H. L., and Hoffman, P. "Sartre's Changed Conception of Consciousness: From Lucidity to Opacity." In *The Philosophy of Jean-Paul Sartre*, edited by P. A. Schilpp. La Salle: Open Court, 1981.

Fleischmann, E. *La Philosophie politique de Hegel*. Paris: Plon, 1964.

Hegel, G. W. F. *Hegel's Philosophy of Nature: Part Two of the Encyclopaedia of the Philosophical Sciences*. Oxford: Clarendon Press, 1970.

————. *Hegel's Philosophy of Mind: Part Three of the Encyclopaedia of the Philosophical Sciences*. Oxford: Clarendon Press, 1971.

————. *Hegel's Philosophy of Right*. Oxford: Oxford University Press, 1967.

————. *Hegel's Science of Logic*. London: George Allen & Unwin; New York: Humanities Press, 1969.

————. "Jenenser Realphilosophie. Philosophie des Geistes." In *Sämtliche Werke, Band XIX*. Leipzig: Meiner, 1932.

————. "Nürnberger Schriften, Bewusstseinslehre und Logik

1808/1809." In *Sämtliche Werke, Band XXI*. Leipzig: Meiner, 1938.

———. *Die Phänomenologie des Geistes*. Hamburg: Meiner, 1952.

———. *The Phenomenology of Mind*. London: George Allen & Unwin; New York: Humanities Press, 1966.

———. "Philosophische Propädeutik." In *Sämtliche Werke, Dritter Band*, Edited by Glockner. Stuttgart: F. Frommans Verlag, 1927.

———. *Reason in History: A General Introduction to the Philosophy of History*. Indianapolis: Bobbs-Merrill, 1953.

Heidegger, M. *Being and Time*. New York: Harper and Row, 1962.

Hobbes, T. *Leviathan*. Baltimore: Pelican, 1968.

Hoffman, P. *The Anatomy of Idealism: Passivity and Activity in Kant, Hegel, and Marx*. The Hague: Martinus Nijhoff, 1982.

———. "The Sensible and the Supersensible in Hegel's Theory of Human Action." *Revue Internationale de Philosophie*, nos. 139–40 (1982): 183–94.

Hyppolite, J. *Genesis and Structure of Hegel's "Phenomenology of Spirit"*. Evanston, Ill.: Northwestern University Press, 1974.

Kant, I. "Critique of Practical Reason." In *Critique of Practical Reason and Other Writings in Moral Philosophy*. Chicago: University of Chicago Press, 1949.

———. *Critique of Pure Reason*. New York: St. Martin's Press, 1965.

Kierkegaard, S. *Fear and Trembling and the Sickness Unto Death*. Princeton: Princeton University Press, 1968.

Kojève, A. *Introduction à la lecture de Hegel*. Paris: Gallimard, 1947.

Merleau-Ponty, M. *Phenomenology of Perception*. London: Routledge & Kegan Paul, 1962.

———. *Sense and Non-Sense*. Evanston: Northwestern University Press, 1964.

Plato, *Parmenides*, In *The Collected Dialogues of Plato*. Princeton: Princeton University Press, 1971.

————. *Sophist. Ed. cit.*

————. *Theaetetus, Ed. cit.*

Sartre, J.-P. *Being and Nothingness.* New York: Philosophical Library, 1956.

Schacht, R. L. "Hegel on Freedom." In *Hegel: A Collection of Critical Essays,* edited by A. MacIntyre. New York: Doubleday, 1972.

Scheler, M. "Tod und Fortleben." In *Gesammelte Werke, Band 10.* Bern: Francke, 1957.

Snell, B. *The Discovery of the Mind.* Oxford: Basil Blackwell, 1953.

Strauss, L. *The Political Philosophy of Hobbes.* Chicago: University of Chicago Press, 1963.

Taylor, C. *Hegel.* Cambridge: Cambridge University Press, 1976.

Index